The New Americans
Recent Immigration and American Society

Edited by
Steven J. Gold and Rubén G. Rumbaut

A Series from LFB Scholarly

Undocumented Latino College Students
Their Socioemotional and Academic Experiences

William Pérez and Richard Douglas Cortés

LFB Scholarly Publishing LLC
El Paso 2011

Copyright © 2011 by LFB Scholarly Publishing LLC
All rights reserved.

Library of Congress Cataloging-in-Publication Data

Pérez, William, 1974-
  Undocumented Latino college students : their socioemotional and academic experiences / William Pérez and Richard Douglas Cortés.
      p. cm. -- (The new Americans: recent immigration and American society)
  Includes bibliographical references and index.
  ISBN 978-1-59332-461-2 (hardcover : alk. paper)
 1. Illegal aliens--Education (Higher)--United States. 2. Hispanic Americans--Education (Higher) 3. Hispanic Americans--Education (Higher)--Social aspects. 4. Hispanic Americans--Social conditions. 5. Hispanic Americans--Social life and customs. I. Cortés, Richard Douglas. II. Title.
  LC3727.P47 2011
  371.829'68073--dc23
                                            2011017859

ISBN 978-1-59332-461-2

Printed on acid-free 250-year-life paper.

Manufactured in the United States of America.

In memory of Tam Tran and Cynthia Felix-Trailblazing and Inspiring Leaders of the DREAM Student Activist Movement.

Table of Contents

List of Tables ix

Acknowledgements xi

CHAPTER 1: Introduction 1

CHAPTER 2: Immigration, Psychosocial Functioning, and Higher
   Education Access 17

CHAPTER 3: Arriving at the Higher Education Gateway:
   Challenges and Barriers 45

CHAPTER 4: Coping, Social Support, And Achievement 63

CHAPTER 5: Institutional Perspective on Students'
   Socioemotional Experiences 85

CHAPTER 6: Conclusion 117

Appendix A: Survey 131

Appendix B: Interview Protocol 153

Appendix C: Scales 157

References 161

Index 183

List of Tables

Table 2.1 Participant Background Information 41

Table 2.2 Interview Participant Demographic Information 43

Table 3.1 Psychosocial Distress 57

Table 4.1 Student Academic Profiles 64

Table 4.2 Academic ability group comparisons 82

Table 5.1 Community College Personnel Interview Participants 87

Acknowledgements

We are greatly indebted to the academic mentors that have supported our scholarship. In particular we would like to thank Ray Buriel, Amado Padilla, Guadalupe Valdés, Danny Solórzano, Daryl Smith, Lourdes Argüelles, and Merril Simon. We would also like to thank all the scholars that have encouraged our undocumented student research and provided thoughtful words of advice and guidance. We specifically express our appreciation to Patricia Gándara, Kris Gutiérrez, Eugene García, Laura Rendón, Amaury Nora, Bill Tierney, Richard Duran, Marjorie Faulstich-Orellana, Janna Shadduck-Hernandez, Raul Hinojosa, Chon Noriega, Vilma Ortiz, Min Zhou, Kent Wong, Victor Narro, Estela Bensimon, Alfred Herrera, Robert Teranishi, Anthony Antonio, H. Sammy Alim, Eamonn Callan, Evelyn Hu-DeHart, Bruce Fuller, Cynthia García Coll, Frances Contreras, Gil Conchas, and Ricardo Stanton-Salazar. We also thank the Claremont Graduate University School of Educational Studies for their unwavering support and assistance disseminating our research findings. In particularly we want to thank dean Margaret Grogan, and all the Education faculty: Deb Smith, Jacob Adams, Scott Thomas, Gail Thompson, Linda Perkins, David Drew, Susan Paik, Phil Drier, Charles Kerchner, Mary Poplin, Barbara DeHart, Carl Cohen, Sue Robb, Delacey Ganley, Anita Quintanar, Jack Shuster, Bruce Matsui, and John Regan.

We greatly appreciate the trust from all the undocumented students who put their apprehensions aside to participate in our research study. We are eternally grateful to our research associates, Karina Ramos and Heidi Coronado who gave their heart and soul to this project and were relentless in their efforts to recruit participants. We also owe a debt of gratitude to Roberta Espinoza for lending her expertise in qualitative methods as well as for the countless hours of editorial support. Thank you to our editors, Professors Steven J. Gold and Rubén G. Rumbaut, for providing us with the opportunity to publish our research under "The New Americans" series. It is both an honor and privilege.

CHAPTER 1
Introduction

Despite their strong belief that the U.S. is the land of opportunity, undocumented immigrants are often stigmatized with labels like "wetbacks," "illegal aliens," and even "criminals." The undocumented community college Latino students we interviewed for this study often described their life as both *cursed and blessed*. One of the students, Guillermo, poignantly captured the general feeling among students about living in the shadows of American society:

> Being an undocumented student in the United States is like being "cursed and blessed" at the same time. Cursed, in that you are marginalized by society, and you have to live in fear almost every day. Blessed, in that you learn from that experience, and you become a much better person because of everything that you have struggled with....You work 10 times as hard as, maybe, somebody who takes it for granted because they were born in this country, or somebody who is a legal resident and doesn't know exactly what that means and the power they have.

Guillermo, who was identified as gifted in elementary school, had no choice but to turn down his offer of admission to the University of California, Berkeley because he did not qualify for federal and institutional financial aid. He tried vigorously to raise money through private scholarships and sponsors to pay for his tuition and housing expenses, but he was unable to come up with the amount he needed. This major setback forced Guillermo to give up his opportunity to attend the best public university in the world. Although extremely difficult, he coped as best as he could with the overwhelming disappointment. He decided to attend his local community college because he knew that it was relatively affordable, and was a stepping-stone to a four-year university.

Historically, students like Guillermo have sought a better life in the U.S. to escape harsh conditions in their country of origin such as armed conflicts, poverty, or political persecution. Many have witnessed or experienced extreme violence and hardship before immigrating (Zea, Diehl, & Porterfield, 1997; Zuniga, 2002). As a result, relative to the conditions they left behind, immigrant parents and their children come to believe that they are fortunate to live in a country that provides more security and opportunities than their country of origin (Suarez-Orozco, 1989; Suarez-Orozco & Suarez-Orozco, 2001).

Growing up in the U.S., however, Latino undocumented students often experience multiple socioemotional and psychosocial challenges that significantly impact their academic and physical well-being. As Zuniga (2002) asserts, "Comprehension of the immigrant experience must consider if, and to what extent, the immigrants have to also address racism and prejudice as they strive to adjust to this new cultural order" (p. 142). Few studies have examined their socioemotional and academic difficulties, particularly after they transition to higher education. In this study, we investigated the unique challenges faced by undocumented Latino community college students. We focused specifically on the community college system as previous research suggests it serves as the primary entry point into higher education for these students (Dozier, 1995; Pérez et al., 2006; Szelenyi & Chang, 2002). As such, our research was guided by the following questions: What are the particular socioemotional experiences of undocumented Latino community college students? How do students cope with socioemotional challenges that result from their legal status? What is the relationship between students' socioemotional experiences and academic outcomes? One of our primary goals was to generate a set of findings that would help to inform educators, administrators, educational researchers, and policymakers regarding the practical, policy, and research implications.

Political context

Over those last three decades, contradictions between the U.S.'s economic and immigration policies have created a growing number of unauthorized migrants. The situation has given rise to an increased number of low-wage laborers to meet the needs of the economy, but without giving workers the protections of legal status. These socio-political processes have also prompted the growth of the number of immigrant children, for whom legal status, poor schools, and poverty make social and economic mobility extremely difficult. Unauthorized immigrants endure increasingly harsh circumstances in this country, including poverty level wages, ICE (Immigration and Control Enforcement) raids at work and home, deportations, and hate crimes. In the absence of national legislation, local municipalities across the country have attempted to pass and enforce ordinances that restrict and criminalize undocumented persons. Meanwhile, anti-immigrant politicians, talk show hosts, and vigilante groups have contributed to growing nativist hysteria. Although nativists' myths affirm the notion that undocumented persons are an extreme burden to society via their use of social services, empirical research proves the contrary. In fact, research has found that less than one percent of immigrants who recently moved to the U.S. did so primarily for the social services, and confusion about eligibility coupled with fear of deportation make immigrants less likely to utilize public resources (Bohrman & Murakawa, 2005).

Decades of failed immigration policies as well as economic push and pull factors have played a central role in increasing the undocumented population in the United States to approximately 12 million as of 2008 (Passel & Cohn, 2009). These numbers include approximately 3.2 million youths under age twenty-four (about one-fourth of the total undocumented population) that were brought by their parents very young, often before schooling age (Hoefer, Rytina, Baker 2009). About three-quarters (76%) of the nation's unauthorized immigrant population are Hispanic consisting of Mexicans, Salvadorans, and Guatemalans ((De Genova, 2004; Passel & Cohn, 2009). The majority of undocumented immigrants (59%) are from Mexico, numbering approximately 7 million. Other significant regional sources of unauthorized immigrants include Asia (11%), Central

America (11%), South America (7%), the Caribbean (4%) and the Middle East (less than 2%). Unauthorized immigrants are now spread more broadly than in the past into states where relatively few had settled two decades ago, including Georgia, North Carolina, and other southeastern states. Despite the growing immigrant diaspora, however, California is still home to the largest number of undocumented immigrants—2.7 million, or 42% of the total U.S. undocumented immigrant population.

Upon arrival, undocumented immigrants are often concentrated in central cities and disproportionately work in low-skill jobs, and on average, have less than a high school education. Their children in turn tend to grow up in neighborhoods and attend schools where they are exposed disproportionately to peer groups involved with youth gangs and intergroup violence. Indeed, an unauthorized status can affect virtually every facet of an immigrant's life—especially during the transition to adulthood (**Rumbaut & Komaie, 2010**). For immigrant young adults, an undocumented status blocks access to the opportunity structure and paths to social mobility. It has become all the more consequential since the passage of draconian federal laws in 1996, the advent of the "war on terror" after September 11, 2001, and the failure by Congress to pass comprehensive immigration reforms.

During times of economic recession, the influx of undocumented immigrants has spurred a gamut of anti-immigrant legislation (Portes & Rumbault, 2006; Suarez-Orozco & Suarez-Orozco, 2001). These efforts are often driven by the belief that undocumented immigrants are responsible for the social and economic problems of American society (Brettell & Sargent, 2006; Chavez, 1991; Zuniga, 2002). Many Americans view immigrants as threats to their social and psychological well-being, social identity, and national economy (Eses, Dovidio, Jackson, & Armstrong, 2001). Anti-immigrant laws often criminalize undocumented individuals, including children whose decision to come here was not their own (Garcia, 1995). The social and political anti-immigrant sentiment causes undocumented students to live on the margins of society and discourages them from pursuing their educational aspirations in order to avoid being further ostracized (Callahan, 2006). A study by Pearson (2010) examined how different terms such as "illegal aliens" or "undocumented workers" invoked different levels of prejudice and found that the term "illegal aliens"

Introduction 5

caused greater prejudice than "undocumented workers," indicating that "illegal aliens" is associated with increased perceptions of threat. The findings suggest that labels used to describe immigrants intensify prejudice and discrimination towards them. In their longitudinal ethnographic work, Portes and Rumbaut (2006) posited that the frequent experiences of social marginality and exclusion may be detrimental to immigrants' socioemotional development. They further argued that a large percentage of newcomers are likely to develop multiple psychological issues because of their deep "sense of estrangement and malaise" (p. 171).

Undocumented young adults are coming of age amid a hostile political backlash and rising animus toward immigrants. In addition, thousands of immigrants have been deported ("removed") over the past decade, with the expansion of the enforcement budget for Immigrations and Customs Enforcement under the newly created Department of Homeland Security. Federal raids of workplaces and private homes and other enforcement campaigns have been intensified, separating families. Hundreds of new laws and ordinances seek to achieve social control at the local level—restricting access to drivers' licenses, education, employment, housing, even library cards. States such as South Carolina have banned all undocumented young adults from the state's community colleges. Not surprisingly, the 2007 National Survey of Latinos found that 53 percent of all Hispanic adults in the United States (about one-fourth of whom are undocumented immigrants) feared that they, a family member, or friend would be deported.

The transition into higher education under these circumstances, is invariably shaped by young adults' legal residency status. Undocumented youth do not qualify for federal financial aid or, in for in-state tuition in all but eleven states. In Arizona, for example, the passage of Proposition 300 in 2006, which restricts in-state tuition and financial aid to legal residents, quickly resulted in a drop in enrollment at local community colleges and public universities. Some 300 students were estimated to have dropped out of the University of Arizona in Tucson, and as many as 1,000 students from Pima Community College were affected by the passage of this new legislation (**Rumbaut & Komaie, 2010**). In California, one of eleven states where undocumented students are allowed to pay in-state tuition, only 1,620 undocumented students were estimated to have enrolled in the

University of California and California State University systems in 2005—a minuscule fraction of the 630,000 students enrolled in the UC and CSU systems, let alone the 2.5 million in all of California's public higher education, including community colleges (Gonzales, 2007).

The Context of Education for Undocumented Students

Undocumented students initially received legal access to K-12 public education as a result of the 1982 Supreme Court case of *Plyler v. Doe*. The Court ruled that undocumented children must be provided access to a free public education because citizens and/or potential citizens cannot achieve any meaningful degree of individual equality without it. The Court held that while undocumented children are present in the United States, they should not forfeit their education because of their parents' decision to immigrate illegally. The Court also indicated that denying education to children who cannot affect their parent's conduct nor their own status would impose a lifetime hardship on them for their disabling status. Educating children regardless of their immigration status, the Court argued, is essential for creating individuals who can function in society and contribute to the development of the U.S.

Presently however, court-mandated equal access to education ends when undocumented students graduate from high school. Each year, between 65,000 and 80,000 undocumented students who have lived in the United States for at least five years become high school graduates, joining the ranks of an estimated 1.7 million undocumented young adults between the ages of 18-24. Upon graduating, and after extensive public educational investment, higher education becomes an elusive dream for these young adults with only 26% of those between ages 18-24 enrolling in college (Fortuny, Capps, Passel, 2007). A recent analysis of college attendance finds that among all undocumented young adults between the ages of 18-24 who have graduated from high school, half (49%) are in college or have attended college. The comparable figure for U.S.-born residents is 71%. Among those ages 18-24, many have not completed high school (40%)—much more than among legal immigrants (15%) or U.S.-born residents (8%). Immigrant children who arrive at a younger age, however, have an increased likelihood of higher educational attainment. Among those who arrived at age 14 or older, 42% are in college or have attended college compared to 61% of those who arrived before age 14 are in college or have attended college. While this "college continuation rate" is higher for unauthorized immigrants who arrive as young children, it is still considerably lower than the rate for legal immigrants (76%) or U.S.-born residents (71%) (Passell & Cohn, 2009).

Despite the efforts of advocates and immigration reform proponents, the federal government has not been able to agree on legislation that would address the legal limbo of undocumented students, particularly the financial hardship they face if they want to pursue a college education. Under current law, they are not eligible to receive state or federal financial aid. In most states they are required to pay international student tuition rates which can be three-to-ten times higher than resident tuition fees. In high immigration areas such as California, with 40% of the total undocumented student population in the nation, undocumented youth may constitute half of senior and graduating high school classes (Johnston, 2000; Leovy, 2001).

Fourteen years after *Plyler v. Doe*, the passage of two bills affected undocumented student access to higher education: the 1996 Personal Responsibility and Work Opportunity Reconciliation Act (PRWORA) and the 1996 Illegal Immigration Reform and Immigrant Responsibility Act (IIRAIRA). PRWORA barred students from access to financial aid for a postsecondary education. Outside of increasing border control, barriers of entry, stipulating additional requirements and extending the citizenship application process and legal penalties as part of larger immigration reform, IIRAIRA reaffirmed a no-access policy regarding any type of public financial aid for undocumented students for higher education. Although the IIRAIRA does not bar undocumented students from attending postsecondary institutions, policymakers are unclear if the law allows for in-state tuition charges for undocumented students. In-state tuition costs have a significant impact on whether undocumented students enroll in a postsecondary institution (Flores & Horn, 2010).

To address the lack of higher education access of undocumented high school graduates, in 2001 Texas, followed by California, Illinois, Kansas, New Mexico, Nebraska, New York, Oklahoma, Utah, Washington, and Wisconsin took matters into their own hands and passed in-state tuition policies that began to open the doors to higher education. Additionally, Texas and New Mexico stand out from the other in-state tuition states in that they also make students eligible for various grants under their state financial aid programs. While undocumented immigrants in these states are allowed to attend public colleges and universities at in-state tuition rates, they are still not able to work due to their undocumented status even if they earn a college degree.

The plight of undocumented students has slowly moved to the forefront of the national debate over immigration reform legislation. As a result of efforts of various organizations across the country that began pressing Congress to introduce federal legislation that would allow undocumented students to obtain legal resident status, the Development, Relief, and Education of Alien Minors (DREAM) Act was introduced in 2001. If passed, the DREAM Act would enable high school graduates to apply for legal conditional status. During this conditional period, undocumented students would be required to attend college and graduate, or serve in the U.S. military for at least two years. If students meet these requirements, they would be granted permanent residency at the end of the conditional period (National Immigration Law Center, 2005; Yates, 2004). Despite a decade of efforts by immigration advocates, in December 2010, the DREAM Act fell five votes short in the Senate from becoming law and thus undocumented students remain in limbo. Their ongoing marginalization continues to be chronicled by countless newspaper stories that describe the impressive academic accomplishments and civic engagement while they struggle to embark or continue with their college education.

Undocumented Immigrant Students

Migration is one of the most radical transitions and life changes an individual or family can endure. For immigrant children, the migration experience fundamentally reshapes their lives as familiar patterns and ways of relating to other people dramatically change. Some potential stressors related to migration include loss of close relationships, housing problems, a sense of isolation, obtaining legal documentation, going through the acculturation process, learning the English language, negotiating their ethnic identity, changing family roles, and adjusting to the schooling experience (Garza, Reyes, & Trueba, 2004; Igoa, 1995; Portes & Rumbaut, 2001a; Suarez-Orozco & Suarez-Orozco, 2001;

Zhou, 1997). Research suggests a host of socio-cultural experiences related to the acculturation process that are extremely stressful for Latino immigrant youth (Cervantes & Castro, 1985). Using the Hispanic Children's Stress Inventory, researchers have identified several potentially stressful events for children and adolescents which include leaving relatives and friends behind when moving, feeling pressured to speak only Spanish at home, living in a home with many people, and feeling that other kids make fun of the way they speak English (Padilla, 1986; Padilla, Cervantes, Maldonado, & Garcia, 1988).

Although there is a growing body of research on first and second generation immigrant youth, there is a dearth of research on undocumented immigrant students. In one of only a handful of studies, Dozier (1993) notes three central emotional concerns for undocumented college students are fear of deportation, loneliness, and depression. Dozier found that students' fear of deportation was so central to undocumented students' daily existence that it influenced almost every aspect of their lives. Some students reported being afraid of going to hospitals because they worried that their immigration status would be questioned. Because their legal status made it impossible to obtain work authorization, they were sometimes forced to stay in bad working conditions because they feared not being able to find another job. Additionally, undocumented students were often reluctant to develop close, emotional relationships with others for fear of their undocumented status being discovered. Despite these stressors, the undocumented students in Dozier's study managed to accumulate the necessary academic record to enroll in college. How did they manage such accomplishments in the face of the many obstacles they describe?

In an ethnographic study of ten undocumented male Mexican college students, they described relationships with school counselors and teachers as being particularly important sources of information and guidance (De Leon, 2005). On the other hand, students also noted teachers who treated them negatively, and similar to Dozier's study, reported an ongoing sense of isolation and fear. Although they recognize all the obstacles they faced due to their undocumented status, participants still expressed a high level of optimism and perseverance. Another qualitative study that focused on undocumented female Mexican college students reports that the young women had both positive and negative experiences with teachers and other school agents (Munoz, 2008). Despite high levels of economic hardship, participants reported high parental involvement and support for school, particularly from mothers. Ethnic identity formation, stereotypes about Mexicans, and negotiating gender role expectations with their parents were described as stressors. All respondents reported frustration, helplessness, shame, and fear due to their undocumented status, but were also highly involved on campus in extracurricular activities as a way to feel a sense of belonging.

Another recent study highlighted undocumented students' various sources of stress and support (Gonzalez, Plata, Garcia, Torres, Urrieta, 2003). A young woman in the study, for example, who grew up in a household with three other siblings and a single mother recalled the pivotal role played by her eighth grade English teacher who recommended her for the Honors program. She eventually participated in various extracurricular activities and aspired for admission to an Ivy League school. In addition to her high level of involvement, her GPA was a stellar 4.38 until she found out she was undocumented. At that point she became disillusioned, discontinued most of her activities, dropped her Honors and AP courses, and let her GPA fall to a 2.5. Another student in the study cites supportive teachers on the one hand, and a lack of support from her high school counselor who questioned her academic abilities and refused to place her in academically rigorous courses on the other.

Oliverez's (2006) qualitative study on Latino undocumented high school seniors finds that although families supported students aspirations to attend college, the high poverty home environments were not always conducive to college preparation. In addition to caring for younger siblings, the crowded nature of their family's small rented apartment meant that students often did their homework away from home, secluded themselves in a corner, or waited until everyone was asleep to get their work done. None of the students had a separate room in their homes where they could find adequate quiet space to study. In all, 60% lived in crowded homes with 6 or more people while 90% lived in single-bedroom or studio apartments where everyone slept in the same room.

Oliverez also found that students were motivated to do well in school by their parents' work ethic. Despite parents' limited education and familiarity with the U.S. educational system, half her participants reported that their parents' hard work and sacrifices motivated them to pursue higher education. Whereas some students attributed their lack of academic success to not having enough time or being too busy to complete their school work to the best of their ability, others held jobs that sometimes left them too tired to focus on school. Sixty percent reported working after school or on the weekends between 16 and 40 hours per week. Their length of time in the U.S. also appeared to play a role in their academic success. Those who had spent 10 years or more in the U.S. had lower GPA's than those who had been in the U.S. for three to eight years. All students reported being frustrated by the numerous restrictions they encountered due to their undocumented status. Similar to findings from another study (Munoz, 2008), 40% chose to be proactive by engaging in community service or mentoring activities to help other undocumented youths.

A study that compared documented and undocumented students similarly reports various environmental risk factors (Abrego, 2006). Both documented and undocumented students reported various incidents of violence near their homes and schools, and attend poorly funded schools with four-year college-going rates of less than 10%. Unlike their counterparts with legal status, undocumented students feared the same fate as their older siblings who excelled in school but ended up in undesirable jobs with few options due to their undocumented status. Some students reported a drop in their academic performance and found it difficult to remain motivated once they learned about their legal status. In fact, many eventually became disillusioned and lowered their life aspirations.

Finally, a recent ethnographic study focusing on fifteen undocumented Latino students in the Midwest finds that despite their legal status, undocumented college students firmly believe in pursing "the American Dream" through schooling and often feel frustrated by efforts to block the Dream Act and other legislation that would provide them with a path to legalization (Morales, Herrera, Murry, 2009). The students in the study credit their parents and their religious convictions as sources of strength. Despite their daily frustrations, participants remain positive and optimistic about their future, and often reframe their negative experiences in positive terms. Additionally, all but two students in the study were actively involved in activism focused on the

Dream Act and immigrant rights. Students reported feeling a sense of empowerment as a result of their activism.

The findings from the few studies focusing on undocumented Latino youths suggest that while both documented and undocumented immigrant Latinos face similar educational and psychological risks, undocumented youth's precarious legal status translates into additional layers of stress and hardship. Sometimes they have supportive teachers that help them overcome various challenges and forge ahead, other times they must contend with teachers that discourage and demoralize them. Undocumented students must also cope with socioeconomic difficulties associated with poverty. The findings from the handful of qualitative studies provide important insights into the educational experiences of undocumented Latino students. However, the psychological and academic effects of legal marginalization have not been fully studied nor addressed by researchers.

Research examining the unique socioemotional issues that undocumented Latino college students experience on a daily basis remains limited. Many of these students encounter various forms of explicit and implicit institutional and personal discrimination, rejection, anxiety, poverty, fear of deportation, pressures of acculturation, and family turmoil, which may inevitably promote high levels of socioemotional and psychosocial distress (Dozier, 1993, 1995; Evans & English, 2002; Finch & Vega, 2003; Garcia Coll & Magnuson, 2005; Portes & Rumbaut, 2001; Suarez-Orozco & Suarez-Orozco, 2001). Very little is known about how receiving society's attitudes and views directly impacts their psychological well-being (Brettell & Sargent, 2006; Zea, Diehl, & Porterfield, 1997; Zuniga, 2002).

Institutional Capacity to Serve Undocumented Students

Despite previous findings, research focused specifically on community college undocumented students remains scarce. There is a need for research on Latino undocumented students at the community college given the rising trend of enrollment noted in both Texas and California (Chavez et al., 2007; Jauregui et al., 2008). In California, the most recent estimates suggests there are about 30,000 undocumented students enrolled in the community college system compared to less than 5,000 enrolled in the University of California and California State

University systems (Chavez et al., 2007). Undocumented students have demonstrated a "mixed pattern of attendance," in which students alternate between full-time or part-time enrollment (Dozier, 2001). The discrepancy has been found to be partially related to lack of funds to pay for full-time enrollment and/or added responsibilities with work or home (Chavez et al., 2007; Dozier, 2001).

The number of undocumented students enrolled in community colleges in the United States has steadily increased due to unprecedented state legislation that allows them to qualify to pay in-state residency (Oliverez, 2006). Inevitably, the increasing enrollment of undocumented students will require changes in enrollment practices and the way student services programs operate (Hagedorn & Cepeda, 2004). Because undocumented students are restricted from receiving federal and state financial aid in most states, student recruitment, retention, resource accessibility, and career advice practices will need to be reconsidered. College administrators, faculty, and staff members have virtually no understanding of the psychosocial and legal hardships undocumented students face. In particular, counselors, teaching faculty, and front-line college personnel need to be informed because they play a vital role in the academic success of students.

As a community college counseling professional for 12 years, one of the co-authors has worked with hundreds of undocumented Latino students who have shared their academic and personal experiences with him. Many of them feel that some faculty and professionals in college student services are not sensitive or adequately trained to deal with their unique situations. In fact, some have reported experiencing discrimination and apathy from college personnel at their respective community college campuses. Often, these institutions lack the awareness, training, and resources necessary to respond effectively to undocumented students' socioemotional and academic needs. Consequently, they fail to cease on the opportunity to further nurture the talents and aspirations of this unique student population (Pérez, 2009, Pérez et al., 2009).

In light of these circumstances, various elements must be considered when working with undocumented students; for example, are college personnel sensitive and adept in working with this population? Are adequate resources in place to facilitate their academic success? Is the community college infrastructure inclusive of this population? In response to these concerns, this study is designed to inform community college educators, general college personnel, and policymakers about the socioemotional experiences that significantly impact undocumented students' academic endeavors and psychological well-being. Understanding their socioemotional issues and common personal characteristics can provide community colleges and other institutions with information that may be helpful in designing or improving existing programs and policies. College practitioners can also use findings from this study to design intervention strategies to help undocumented community college students seek academic and personal support without trepidation or anxiety.

Organization of the book

Undocumented Latino community college students experience multiple layers of social and psychological threat (e.g., social marginalization, discrimination, and stress) that can negatively impact their well-being. Currently, little is known about how they deal with anti-immigrant sentiment and policies that directly prevent them from accessing higher education. In recent years, there has been an increase in undocumented students attending community colleges due to state legislation that allows them to qualify for in-state resident tuition rates if they meet certain criteria (Oliverez, 2006). However, undocumented students are still restricted from receiving federal and state financial aid in most states, which poses great financial and emotional hardships. These conditions have created the need for a thorough understanding of their socioemotional and academic experiences (Dozier, 1993). In this book we examined how undocumented Latino students cope with the challenges created by their legal status. Chapter 2 provides a review of the literature on the socioemotional and psychological well-being of undocumented immigrants, presents the socioemotional framework that guides our study, and describes an overview of the data collection methods and analyses. Using a mixed-methods approach that included both qualitative and quantitative data, we examined the socioemotional and academic experiences of currently-enrolled community college students. Chapter 3 examines the wide range of socioemotional challenges that undocumented community college Latino students face on a regular basis due to their status. Results suggest that undocumented Latino community college students experience social rejection, distress, and anxiety, yet, depression levels remain moderately low in spite of various socioemotional pressures. Chapter 4 gives an in-depth description of the ways in which students cope with adversity, including a discussion of the role of social support systems that help students remain academically engaged. This chapter also discusses the pivotal role that community colleges play in providing undocumented students with primary access to higher education due to their low tuition cost. Chapter 5 focuses on the perspectives of community college personnel who work with undocumented students. Community college personnel confirm both the challenges and sources of support described by undocumented Latino students. The findings highlight the important role of student advocates on campus, as well as the need for training and professional development instruction for community college personnel at all levels to better understand and serve undocumented students. The conclusion chapter provides a discussion of the socioemotional implications of the ongoing legal marginality of undocumented Latino students. It makes suggestions for how the community college administration, faculty, and support staff can assist undocumented Latino community college students as well as recommendations for future research and policy.

CHAPTER 2

Immigration, Psychosocial Functioning, and Higher Education Access

Research on immigrant mental health indicates that recent immigrants tend to have fewer mental health issues compared to their American-born peers, but these trends change over time (Escobar et al., 2000; Gee, Ryan, & Laflamme et al., 2006). In fact, among immigrant Latino families, acculturation, parental educational attainment, and socioeconomic status are correlated with depression (Araujo & Borrell, 2006; Berry, 1990; Finch & Vega, 2003; Portes & Rumbaut, 2006; Rivera, 2007). Gee at al. (2006) finds that immigrants develop more psychological symptoms with increased time in the U.S. as a result of their daily experiences of racial discrimination and unfair treatment. Higher rates of suicide and substance abuse have been found among immigrants with greater length of residence in the U.S. (Burnam et al., 1987; Finch, Kolody, & Vega, 2000; Portes & Rumbaut, 2006). Considering the limited accessibility to adequate health care, undocumented families may be further at risk (Chavez et al., 1997; Ponce, Nordyke, & Hirota, 2005).

Undocumented immigrants may have distinct characteristics compared to either their documented immigrant or American counterparts. Is documentation status related to mental health, and if so, why and how? Is "undocumentedness" a higher-risk category in comparison to documented immigrants? Should documentation status be considered in the assessment of psychological and emotional well-being? Though few studies have examined the impact of legal status on immigrant families, findings suggest that it can shape migration and acculturation experiences and influence the risk of depression and anxiety. The limited research available suggests that undocumented adult Mexican immigrants are more likely to experience a traumatic event, have fewer economic and social resources, and are more marginalized and vulnerable to exploitation (Sullivan & Rehm, 2005).

Studies of undocumented Latino immigrants in the United States and Canada find that perceptions of social isolation and the uncertainty related to their undocumented status add to the stress associated with the immigration experience (Chavez, 1991; Hagan, Rodriguez, Capps, & Kabiri, 2003; Simich, 2006). Compared with documented Latino immigrants, undocumented immigrants are more likely to live alone or separated from members of their nuclear family and to report lower proficiency in English (Arbona, Olvera, Rodriguez, Hagan, Linares, & Wiesner (2010). Fear of deportation, in addition to being a source of stress and anxiety, may discourage undocumented immigrants from seeking help for employment, health, and language skill difficulties they encounter (Rodriguez & Hagan, 2004; Simich, 2006; Sullivan & Rehm, 2005), further compounding the stress they experience related to immigration-related challenges. For example, Arbona et al. (2010) found that about one-third of the undocumented Latino immigrants in their study reported that they avoided activities such as walking in the street or requesting services from government agencies for fear of deportation. Fear of deportation was the strongest predictor of extra- and intrafamilial acculturative stress among undocumented immigrants. Being undocumented may also impact men and women differently. Arbona, et al. (2010) found that men were more likely than women to be undocumented, to be separated from their nuclear families, and reported higher levels of extrafamilial stress, and greater fear of deportation. These findings are similar to a qualitative study that revealed that undocumented Latino immigrants were primarily male and Spanish speaking and were more likely to report lack of family support than documented immigrants (Pérez & Fortuna, 2005).

The literature suggests that undocumented immigrants do have a unique risk profile, which may contribute to different mental health outcomes as compared to their documented counterparts. After arriving in the United States, legal status and discrimination emerge as significant stressors and become important determinants of mental health outcomes. In a study of the impacts of acculturation stress and social support on immigrants' perceived health status, Finch and Vega (2003) found "legal status stress" to have a significant effect. Defined as an acculturation stressor, legal status stress was measured by fear of deportation and its consequences, avoidance of immigration officials, difficulty finding legal services, and limited contact with family and friends because of legal status. While acculturation stressors in general were moderately associated with poorer health, legal status stress alone significantly increased the likelihood of rating one's health as fair/poor. Cavazos-Rehg et al. (2007) hypothesized that undocumented status is a "persistent and insidious psycho environmental stressor" that increases Latino immigrants' vulnerability to acculturative stress and other socioemotional problems. Their findings showed that Latino immigrants concerned with deportation reported higher levels of extrafamilial acculturative stress (stress related to economic and occupational challenges) than immigrants who did not express deportation concerns.

The studies that have been conducted on undocumented Mexican immigrants demonstrate that compared to their documented counterparts, they are pervasively affected by exploitation and vulnerability; physical, mental, and emotional hardships; lower and uncertain wages, lower employment status, fewer kinship networks, less English proficiency, less education, and poorer housing; less health insurance coverage, access to care, and quality of care; a fear of deportation that prevents some from seeking medical care; and the leading of "secret lives" (Cornelius, 1982; Ku & Waidman, 2003; Moore, 1986; Chavez, 1991; Messias, 1996; Pickwell & Warnock, 1994; Chavez, Cornelius, & Jones, 1986; Cornelius, Chavez, & Jones, 1984; Berk & Schur, 2001; Weintraub, 2003).

In addition to dangerous border crossings, limited resources, and restricted mobility, undocumented Mexican immigrants experience a unique sense of marginalization and isolation. Media portrayal and society attitudes play a significant role in stigmatizing them that can erode self-worth and potentially lead to depression. Undocumented Mexican immigrants are frequently scapegoated, discriminated against, and treated as deviants. The psychological burden of being blamed and stigmatized by media and the larger society is manifested in the daily experiences, perceptions, and actions of undocumented Mexican immigrants. Thus, they are at risk of low self-esteem, guilt, shame, fear, and insecurity (Hall, Stevens, & Meleis, 1994; Arias, 1981; Dumon, 1983; Ureta, 2001). In sum, there is an emerging picture in the literature of the increased psychological burden of being an undocumented Mexican immigrant in American society. Stressful experiences include living in a hostile environment, fear of deportation, and states of hyper-vigilance (Guttmacher, 1983; McGuire & Georges, 2003; Smart & Smart, 1995). They have reported loneliness, disorientation, isolation, feeling trapped, depression, and sadness. Their marginality is reinforced by the ambiguousness of being "illegal" on one hand, while being unofficially welcomed through the economic "back door" on the other (Hall, Stevens, Meleis, 1994; McGuire & Georges, 2003). These ongoing stressful experiences exacerbate health risks (McGuire & Georges, 2003; Ureta, 2001). In addition, undocumented Mexican immigrants experiences of discrimination result in questioning self-worth, which may increase their risk of depression (Arias, 1981). Overall, these findings suggest that in the social environment created by restrictive immigration legislation, fear of deportation contributes the most to acculturative stress among Latino immigrants. This fear is associated with increased acculturative stress in both the extrafamilial and intrafamilial contexts above and beyond the stress associated with immigration-related challenges such as separation from family and language difficulties.

Despite these findings, the long-term effects of fear of deportation on the psychological functioning of Latino immigrants and their families remain unknown. It is reasonable to expect that long-term exposure to stress associated with fear of deportation is likely to have a negative impact on an individual's thoughts, emotions, and social functioning. Although no major changes in immigration law have been enacted since 1996, in recent years state and local governments have greatly intensified the enforcement of these laws. For example, deportations increased by more than fivefold between 1996 and 2008 (U.S. Department of Homeland Security, 2009, table 36). The 2008 national survey conducted by the Pew Hispanic Center indicated that in the past year, Latino respondents had observed more frequent involvement of local police in the questioning of Latinos about their legal status, and more frequent workplace raids by government agents (Pew Hispanic Center, 2009). Stricter enforcement of the immigration laws and higher deportation rates of Latino immigrants have resulted in higher levels of family separation, fear, and stress among Latinos, particularly undocumented immigrants (Hagan & Rodriguez, 2002; N. Rodriguez & Hagan, 2004). Rutter (1988) posits that coping is the dual function of problem-solving and regulation of emotional distress. Mexican immigrants are more likely use positive reframing, denial, and religion, while they are less likely to use substance abuse and self-distraction as coping mechanisms (Farley, Galves, Dickinson, & Diaz-Pérez, 2005). In another study, Zea, Diehl, and Porterfield (1997) found that Mexican and Central American immigrants were able to cope with trauma and depression by employing three protective factors: social support, psychosocial competence, and cognitive factors. By relying on both their psychosocial competence and cognitive abilities, they applied various problem-solving skills to manage their distress and trauma. In a study examining acculturation, legal status, and perceived discrimination stressors, Finch and Vega (2003) reported that Latino immigrants were able to buffer these social challenges with the support of family members and significant others (e.g., peers, teachers, and community leaders). Results showed that participants reported better physical and psychosocial conditions when linked with high levels of social and emotional support.

Undocumented Adolescents and Young Adults

Undocumented immigrants in the U.S. often struggle finding stable employment and housing due to their immigration status (Finch & Vega, 2003). These kinds of social barriers can perpetuate an inevitable cycle of poverty, including poor mental and physical health (Callahan & Ragan, 2006; Finch & Vega, 2003; Portes & Rumbaut, 2006). When they arrive, new immigrants tend to settle in urban neighborhoods with high concentrations of poverty and accompanying social ills such as violence and poor sanitary conditions (Orfield & Yun, 1999). In addition, undocumented immigrants often experience distress, fear, and imprisonment because of the potential risk of being apprehended by U.S. Customs and Border officials (Chavez, 1991). The fear of deportation can cause anxiety among undocumented families, and is a constant threat to their emotional health (Zuniga, 2002), particularly for immigrant youth. For example, Chavez (1998) reports children being harassed and detained by police and border agents at random bus stops simply because they looked Latino. In these environments, immigrant youth often feel a sense of imprisonment and paranoia (Suarez-Orozco, 2005). Immigration raids by U.S. Immigration and Custom Enforcement agents and the fear of raids can further traumatize children and their parents (Capps et al., 2005). Even children who are citizens, but whose parents or siblings are undocumented (i.e., children in mixed status families), can suffer from the stresses associated with documentation status. Yet few studies have examined how the unique risks of undocumented immigrants—especially adolescents—affect overall mental health (Sullivan & Rehm, 2005).

In one of the few studies, Potochnik and Perreira (2010) found that mental health stressors were prevalent in the lives of first-generation Latino immigrants. Three-quarters of immigrant adolescents had been separated from their primary caregiver prior to their migration, and the average separation period lasted 3 years. During their journey to the United States, nearly a quarter (24%) experienced a stressful migration event. After migration, undocumented status was a common stressor among first-generation Latino youth. Compared with documented adolescents, undocumented adolescents were at greater risk of anxiety, and children in mixed-status families were at greater risk of both anxiety and depressive symptoms. Moreover, immigrant Latino adolescents experienced (42%) and perceived discrimination in their lives. The researchers also found that social supports such as familism and teacher support reduced the odds of depressive symptoms but had no impact on anxiety symptoms. Personal motivation reduced the risk of both symptoms of depression and anxiety. After controlling for the presence of multiple stressors, they also found that experiencing discrimination was significantly associated with an increased likelihood of depressive symptoms. Similarly, after controlling for the presence of multiple supports, they found that years in the United States was significantly associated with decreased likelihood of depressive symptoms.

Most undocumented immigrant youth have been raised in the United States for a significant part of their lives, and as a result, many identify with being American (Pérez, 2009). They have developed a preference for the English language and are accustomed to the American way of life. However, as much as they would like to feel they are part of society, they are also forced to contend with a multiplicity of social stigmas that are reinforced by media images and anti-immigrant rhetoric (Brettel & Sargent, 2006; Pérez, 2009; Padilla & Pérez, 2003).

The sense of estrangement and cultural conflict has a direct correlation to immigrants' sense of identity and connection (Chavez, 1998; Souto-Manning, 2007; Zuniga, 2002). In particular, changes in roles and status, language usage, and the constant exposure to discrimination are all significant factors (Zuniga, 2002). At a very young age, undocumented immigrant children learn about discrimination, fear, and hatred (Chavez, 1991). They are exposed to images and messages that portray undocumented immigrants as criminals and social threats to the U.S., rather than as contributing members of society (Chavez, 1998). These experiences no doubt limit their opportunities for a healthy identity development.

Immigrants' phenotype may also determine the amount of discrimination they will experience in their lifetime. Padilla and Pérez (2003) posit that "persons who are more identifiable as outsiders are more likely to be targets of prejudice and discrimination by the socially dominant in-group" (p. 44). Ethnic identity scholars suggest that identity formation of immigrants is an interaction between the attitudes and characteristics of immigrants and the responses of the receiving society (Phinney, Horenczyk, Liebkind, & Vedder, 2001). Hence, the identity development of undocumented Latino immigrant individuals may be more adversely affected because they are likely to be exposed to social rejection and social stigma due to their legal and minority status, phenotype, accents, and socioeconomic situation (Padilla & Pérez, 2003; Phinney et al., 2001).

Undocumented students may also struggle with conflicting age role expectations (Martinez, 2009). In discussing the contradictions surrounding age roles of Mexican undocumented immigrant teens in the United States, Allison and Takei (1993) describe a Mexican undocumented immigrant child who works in a full time job, like an adult, to support his extended family while being treated like an older child in school (Burton et al., 1996). Levitt (2001) noted that family expectations caused teenage immigrants in Boston to work full-time and use their earnings to support their siblings' extended schooling participation, effectively limiting their own adolescence. In experiencing these contradictory roles and expectations, scholars suggest that youth feel compelled to choose between roles, and ultimately life stages, more often opting to transition to adulthood at earlier ages.

Studies on immigrant achievement motivation have suggested that work ethic and motivation in students is attributed to the *"dual frame of reference"* paradigm (Ogbu, 1986, 1991; Suarez-Orozco & Suarez-Orozco, 1995). The dual frame of reference is an immigrants' retrospective outlook comparing their previous difficult living conditions in their native countries to their present living circumstances in the U.S. For example, it is a common practice for immigrant parents to express to their children that they are fortunate to live in a country that offers more opportunities. As a result, immigrant children may become more likely to value schooling (Gallimore & Reese, 1999; Portes & Rumbaut, 2001). In addition to a dual frame of reference, family obligation is also strongly linked to achievement motivation (Fuligni, 1997; Pérez, 2004). Immigrant students are often motivated to do well in school because of the sacrifices made by their immigrant parents to provide a better life for them. For undocumented students, however, once they reach their senior year of high school, a different kind of reality begins to materialize as a new sense of "fragility" emerges (Pérez, 2009; Gonzales, 2010).

The Community College as Gateway and Gatekeeper

Even with the moral and academic support from parents, peers, and institutional agents, undocumented college students cannot escape the financial burdens and immigration policies that hamper their chances to pursue a selective four-year postsecondary education (Johnston, 2000b; Perry, 2006). Their sense of accomplishment and optimism may be negatively affected when they are hindered from receiving college scholarships as well as federal and state financial assistance (Johnston, 2000; Allen, 2006; Oliverez, 2006). Many, in fact, automatically disqualify themselves internally from pursuing postsecondary cducation (Johnston, 2000b).

Despite in-state tuition legislation, the public community college system remains the most financially viable route to higher education for undocumented Latino students (Dozier, 1993; Szelényi & Chang, 2002). Historically, public community colleges have been referred to as the "people's colleges," due in part to their long history of educating traditionally excluded working-class and racial minority groups (McGrath & Van Buskirk, 1999). Most of these students enroll at these institutions for their less scrutinizing admission policies and physical proximity (Jenkins, 2003; Kurlaender, 2006).

Since their initial founding more than 100 years ago, community colleges have focused on access, educational opportunity, and workforce preparation (Cohen & Brawer, 2003). Although these institutions have also been charged with preparing students for transfer to baccalaureate programs they are also expected to be the primary providers of workforce preparation at the postsecondary level. Their low tuition, convenient locations, and wide selection of vocational programs make them an attractive option for a diverse population that might otherwise not be able to attend college (Barry & Barry, 1992; Bauer, 1994; Bernstein, 1986; Fields, 1962; Kintzer, 1970, 1973, 1996; Kintzer & Wattenbarger, 1985; Knoell, 1966; Knoell & Medsker, 1965; Phillippe & Sullivan, 2005; Rifkin, 1996; Witt, Wattenbarger, Gollanttscheck, & Suppiger, 1994). Thus, for many, community colleges seemingly serve as the gateway to the baccalaureate.

Unfortunately, studies dating back to the 1970s indicate sharp declines on transfer rates from two-year to four-year colleges which inevitably result in fewer students achieving the baccalaureate degree when commencing postsecondary studies at community colleges (Brint & Karabel, 1989; California Community Colleges, 1994; Dougherty, 1992, 1994; Fields, 1962; Grubb, 1991; Koltai, 1981; Lombardi, 1979; Pascarella & Terenzini, 1991; Pincus, 1980; Pincus & Archer, 1989). The decline in transfer rates fell from 57% in 1970–1971 to 28% in 1984–1985 (Barry and Barry, 1992). Although the transfer rates have been relatively stable for the past 20 years, they have been far from impressive; and such data call into question the characterization of community colleges as accessible paths toward the baccalaureate degree. In 2003, the national average for transfer rates from two-year to four-year institutions was estimated to be 28.9% (U.S. Department of Education, 2003).

As a result of their mixed legacy, community colleges have been characterized as both the gateways and gatekeepers of American higher education. As gateways, they are open-access colleges with minimal enrollment requirements and low tuition. They offer a "something for everyone" curriculum, including occupational certificate programs, general education credits toward the completion of an associate's degree and for transfer to four-year colleges, developmental (or remedial) education, English-language instruction, and noncredit short courses for business training, self-improvement, or leisure (Bragg, 2001; Dougherty, 2002). Currently, they enroll nearly eight million students and about 40 percent of all undergraduates (Horn & Nevill, 2006). However, as a route from the lowest rung to the highest rungs of higher education, transfer primarily serves students of middle and high socioeconomic status (SES) (Dowd et al., 2006). Only a very small proportion (7%) of community college students who transferred to highly selective institutions are students from low SES families. On average, the academic and social characteristics of the eventual transfers closely resembled those of their counterparts who had entered a four-year college directly after high school. The more socially and academically disadvantaged students, who need but are not empowered by their community college experience, are less likely to transfer. Thus, despite the symbolic and structural emphasis on the gateway role of community colleges, some scholars have argued that the real function of the community college is to act as a gatekeeper (Brint & Karabel, 1989). Latino students are greatly affected by this trend (Nora & Rendón, 1990; Pincus & Archer, 1989).

Latinos are disproportionately enrolled in two-year colleges (Chronicle of Higher Education, 2001; Nora, Rendón, & Cuadraz, 1999). In 1996-1997, 70% of Hispanics were enrolled in community colleges compared to 69% of African Americans, and 60% of Whites. In fall of 2000, 58% of Latinos enrolled in college were attending two-year institutions compared to 42% of African American and 36% of White students (Harvey, 2003). Research also suggests that community colleges have not served as the gateway to a bachelor's degree for large numbers of lower-income and ethnic minority populations (Hoachlander, Sikora, Horn, & Carroll, 2003; Wassmer, Moore, & Shulock, 2004). Approximately 25% of Latino students in the Beginning Postsecondary Students Longitudinal Study who attended a two-year college initially intended to transfer to a four-year institution and obtain a bachelor's degree. However, six years after first enrolling in community colleges only 6% had been awarded a bachelor's degree (Hoachlander et al., 2003).

In 2002, only about 10% of Latinos who completed high school continued on to college within a year or two of graduation, and these youth were more likely to enroll in community colleges and attend part-time (Fry, 2002). In fall 2004, nearly 2 million Latinos were enrolled in degree-granting programs in American colleges and universities (12.5% of all students). Community colleges enrolled more than 972,400 of these students—the largest minority group (15% of all enrollments) in those institutions (NCES, 2006).

Latinos are also much more likely to attend less selective institutions, particularly community colleges, regardless of their socioeconomic background or prior academic preparation and achievement (Fry, 2004). In 2003-2004, only 37.7% of college-bound Latinos enrolled in baccalaureate programs, whereas 39.8% enrolled in associate degree programs (both transfer and applied), 10.2% in certificate programs, and 12.3% in non-degree programs (Horn, Nevill, & Griffith, 2006). In community colleges, they enroll more frequently in occupational programs or non-degree tracks than in programs leading to transfer (Horn et al., 2006). Therefore, although the choice to attend a community college might be positive in providing access at a reasonable cost and an environment where other Latinos are enrolled, there are also drawbacks with regard to less rigorous program choices and likelihood of transfer and degree completion.

Latino community college students experience several significant barriers in transferring to four-year institutions. First, they and their parents are not familiar with higher education and have little or no knowledge of academic requirements and procedures (High-Quality Learning Conditions, 2002; Jun, 2001; Martin, 1999; McDonough, 1997; Tornatzky, Cutler, & Lee, 2002). Second, these students typically lack adequate high school preparation (Fry, 2004; Swail, Cabrera, & Lee, 2004; Wellman, 2002). They enroll in academic courses or college preparatory courses at lower rates than their White and Black peers (Latinos in Education, 1999). Third, many immigrants, have limited facility with English, and instruction and tutoring are usually delivered in English (The High-Quality Learning, 2002). Fourth, Latino students work to survive and help support their families and thus may prioritize work over school due to economic necessity (Bean & Eaton, 2000; Bean & Metzner, 1985; Hagedorn, Maxwell, Chen, Cypers, & Moon, 2002; High-Quality Learning Conditions, 2002; Salinas & Llanes, 2003). Fifth, many Latino students who transfer experience difficulty in adjusting to colleges that lack racial or ethnic diversity (Laanan, 2001; Lee 2001; Zamani, 2001). Lastly, numerous institutional barriers impede transfer including relatively few faculty and staff role models (High-Quality Learning Conditions, 2002; Lee, 2001; Pérez, 1999), lack of counseling and orientation (High-Quality Learning Conditions, 2002; Pérez, 1999), prejudice on the part of faculty, and limited transfer programs (High-Quality Learning Conditions, 2002; Lee, 2001).

There is very little research that focuses particularly on the experience of immigrants in community colleges. The City University of New York (CUNY) analysts have conducted some research on the experience of immigrants in the university, including some analysis of the differences among two- and four-year institutions (City University of New York, 1995). Their report notes that more than one-third of the first-time CUNY freshmen in 1990 were foreign-born, while only about 28% of the city's population was not born in the U.S. Native-born children of immigrants—particularly second generation youth—were found to enroll in college at continually higher rates and rapidly overtaking the 46% participation rate for Whites (Fry, 2002).

As a whole, foreign-born students are *not* any more concentrated in two-year programs than they were in CUNY in general (Bayley & Weininger, 2002). It is important to note that the foreign-born are not a homogeneous group. Immigrants at CUNY who attended high school outside of the United States were more likely than foreign-born students educated here to enroll in an associate degree program. One of the most striking findings in this study is that immigrant students are actually overrepresented among the CUNY students relative to their share of the population. While the foreign-born share of the population was just over 40% in 1999, their share of CUNY enrollments was 48% in 1997. Immigrant two-year entrants do appear to have higher levels of educational achievement than natives who enter the same programs. Irrespective of where they attended high school, immigrants earn more credits and are more likely to complete an associate degree. Additionally, immigrants who went to a U.S. high schools were more likely than native-born two-year entrants to transfer to a bachelor's program (Bayley & Weininger, 2002).

The Post-Secondary Challenges of Undocumented College Students

Despite their promise as the gateway to higher education for undocumented students, undocumented students who enroll in community colleges often encounter academic and socioemotional challenges that require special attention, and often go unaddressed (Brilliant, 2000; Dozier, 1993, 1995). In a study focusing on the perception community college personnel have of undocumented students, Jauregui and Slate (2009) note wide variability in academic achievement among community college undocumented students. Whereas some were high academic achievers and more motivated to succeed than students who were U.S. citizens, others had similar academic qualities as their average high school peer graduates, including areas of general academic deficiencies. Undocumented students also arrived at the community college with varying educational backgrounds and differing levels of English proficiency, including many who had spent a significant part of their primary and secondary schooling in Mexico.

According to community college personnel, communication is a crucial element in getting undocumented students to apply, self-identify, enroll, and receive financial aid to pay for classes (Jauregui & Slate, 2009). The ability to communicate in more than one language, in this cases Spanish, was beneficial to undocumented students and their accompanying families in the pre-enrollment process. Participants in the study also revealed communication did not come easy when having considered the dissenting public view about illegal immigration and educating undocumented students. Moreover, fearing undocumented students unwilling to self-disclose their situations created a challenge for college representatives in helping to assisting them.

Jauregui and Slate (2009) also found that sometimes misinformation hindered the admission process of undocumented students and often stalled their efforts to pursue a postsecondary education. For example, one of the participants in their study explained that a recruiter inquired about the legality of undocumented students attending the community college because he heard from a high school counselor that it was illegal for undocumented students to attend. Consequently, the high school counselor was informing undocumented students they could not attend postsecondary institutions (Jauregui & Slate, 2009).

Another challenge for undocumented community college students is weak institutional support due to a lack of awareness about the need for specialized services for undocumented students. When asked about institutional commitment to serve undocumented students, Jauregui and Slate (2009) found that community college personnel felt that institutional efforts to provide equal educational opportunity for all students was sufficient. Most felt that students were being sufficiently served by existing services targeting students with similar background characteristics. Therefore, services and specific assistance to undocumented students were not deemed necessary. Many reported that undocumented students received equal treatment as other students and felt that undocumented students should not receive preferential treatment in the classroom nor in college services.

Other institutional factors can also impact the access, persistence, and educational achievement of undocumented students. Lack of financial aid is one of the biggest barriers (Badger et al., 2000; Jauregui & Slate, 2009). The few existing financial aid resources for which undocumented students qualify is not enough to support undocumented students' quest for a postsecondary education. Another potential barrier is additional academic program prerequisites, such as the requiring of security background checks to selective programs. These policies are a problem for undocumented students because they do not have a social security number. Thus, there needs to be institutional commitment, communication and awareness, and financial aid to assist undocumented students in postsecondary education.

Undocumented students attending Texas borderland community colleges were viewed by college personnel as being highly motivated, having strong regard for family, coming from low socioeconomic backgrounds, but attending school with great fear (Slate & Jauregui, 2009). All of these non-institutional attributes were viewed by community college personnel as impacting undocumented student persistence and educational achievement. Undocumented students were perceived as fearful and in most cases do not self-disclose their situations, making it difficult for college representatives to assist them.

Family was perceived as motivating students to succeed and at times providing a support network. Undocumented students viewed education as the change catalyst for improving the family's quality of life. These students were willing to go to great lengths in sacrificing for the good of the family (Slate & Jauregui, 2009). Campa (2010) also finds that undocumented students' critical resilience is promoted by focusing on the cultivation of a larger purpose connected to the social uplift of their families and communities. These findings are consistent with previous research that finds a relationship between student characteristics, retention, and educational achievement (Garza &Landeck, 2004; Schuetz, 2005; Summers, 2003).

Undocumented students also face various challenges in their career exploration process (Ortiz & Hinojosa, 2010). A key feature in nearly all career development theories is the assertion that making a career choice fundamentally relies on the match between the student's skills, values, and dispositions and the characteristics of the career or job setting—presuming that a match between the individual and the career will result in career success and satisfaction (Holland, 1985). Super (1984) explains that individuals' ability to envision themselves in a career and understand what role they can play in the workplace are important in solidifying career choice and enacting the career decision. However, these general career development concepts may not be compatible with undocumented students since they do not have the freedom to choose and achieve career goals because all elements of the career exploration process are influenced daily by their lack of legal status.

Aside from financial aid, undocumented students do not have legal documentation to work in the United States, which limits their potential to earn income while in college. With the increasing costs of higher education and living expenses, it is no surprise that most undocumented students attend two-year colleges (Diaz-Strong and Meiners, 2007). Lack of employment opportunities after college graduation can be an additional obstacle, even while a student struggles to earn a degree. These legal barriers create an undue burden on students that can have a negative effect on their academic achievement. In short, the financial pressures and lack of opportunities facing undocumented students while in and immediately following college mean that they must work harder to finance their education for a promise of future opportunity that may go unfulfilled.

Socioemotional Framework

The analyses presented in this book are guided by the socioemotional framework (Becker & Luthar, 2002; Santrock, 1997). Scholars have used the socioemotional development framework to examine how an individual's immediate environment impacts his or her emotional and psychological development (Santrock, 1997). According to Santrock, the socioemotional process involves changes in the individual's relationships with other people, changes in emotions, and changes in personality. Based on Erikson's (1997) psychosocial/socioemotional paradigm, socioemotional functioning is shaped by interactions with others (e.g., family, teachers, peers, neighbors) that trigger emotional responses such as anger, anxiety, aggression, assertiveness, depression, fear, joy, or optimism (Bandura, 2001; Erikson, 1997; Santrock, 1997).

For undocumented students, their socioemotional development is not only impacted by the typical environmental factors (e.g., poverty, violence, lack of resources, discrimination) that affect a large percentage of minority children (Kozol, 1991, 2005), but also by additional systemic barriers that prevent them from enjoying all of the social resources available to American citizens and those with legal status. Understanding the patterns of unique psychological processes that relate to undocumented immigrant students' academic and socioemotional functioning can offer new perspectives that can inform student development and achievement motivation theories.

In our analyses we also applied the, Marginality and Mattering framework (Schlossberg, 1989) to guide our understanding on how school social and environmental factors influence the development of undocumented college students. Schlossberg (1989) argues that when students feel marginalized, it can lead to a sense of "self-consciousness, irritability, and depression." On the other hand, feeling that one matters can create a sense of importance or appreciation. Helping undocumented students feel valued, appreciated, and that they matter, despite their immigration status may be key to promoting their academic success.

Previous research also finds that the socioemotional health of students is a significant element to understanding achievement performance (Becker & Luthar, 2002). In a study that examined the relationship between academic achievement and mental health, Roeser, Eccles, and Strobel (1998) found that both internalized distress, such as sadness, anxiety, shame, and guilt that are directed toward the self, and externalized distress such as anger, frustration, and fear directed against others were associated with academic difficulties (Roeser et al., 1998). These types of socioemotional conditions are often-neglected precursors to poor achievement performance and motivation (Becker and Luthar, 2002). In the context of undocumented community college Latino college students, we hypothesized that recurring experiences of marginalization, discrimination, and social rejection would be related to negative socioemotional wellbeing and low academic performance. We closely examined various factors linking socioemotional functioning, the socioecological context, and academic performance.

Undocumented community college students may experience depression, particularly those who were originally admitted to prestigious or reputable 4-year institutions but were unable to attend due to cost (Johnston, 2000a, 2000b; Oliverez, 2006). In addition, for those who come from poorly funded, overcrowded schools—which is commonly the case for undocumented Latino students—the issues of poor college preparedness and English language proficiency often emerge as they begin their community college studies (Brilliant, 2000; Jenkins, 2003; Kurlaender, 2006). Undocumented community college students may feel overwhelmed with feelings of anxiety, mistrust, and fear because they do not feel well connected to their new environment (Dozier, 1993). Further contributing to these emotions are students' perceptions of the lack of institutional commitment to implement effective resources and policies that can meet their academic and psychosocial needs, such as validation, sense of belonging, or positive self-concept (Ornelas & Solorzano, 2004; Rendón, 1994; Suarez, 2003).

Researchers have argued that a strong supportive network at the educational institution level is vital to addressing some of the academic, emotional, and psychosocial concerns of Latino immigrant students (Stanton-Salazar and Dornbusch, 1995). These students must have a deep sense of connection and trust (i.e., *confianza*) in their respective institutional agents in order to feel comfortable enough to seek help (Stanton-Salazar, 2001). Previous scholars have suggested incorporating an ecological approach to understanding the unique socioemotional development and academic functioning of undocumented students (Conye & Cook, 2004; Zuniga, 2002). Although a considerable amount of research has focused on the educational, socioemotional, and psychosocial factors of Latino college students (Conchas, 2001, 2006; Evans & English, 2002; Lopez, 2003; Suarez-Orozco & Suarez-Orozco, 2001; Stanton-Salazar, 2001; Valenzuela, 2003), researchers have devoted little attention to undocumented Latino students' socioemotional issues. With the exception of Dozier (1993) who wrote one of the first empirical articles that focused on the emotional concerns of undocumented community college students, most of the research on undocumented students has focused on immigration policies, socioeconomic conditions, and historical analyses (Chavez, 1998; Chavez, Hubbell, Mishra, & Valdez, 1997; Olivas, 2004; Oliverez, 2006

The Study

The process set in motion by the 1982 federal ruling calling for a national guarantee of basic education to all students regardless of immigration status has nurtured a generation of undocumented students who are coming of age, graduating from U.S. high schools, and are seeking the next level of opportunity. Presently, however, court-mandated equal access to education ends when undocumented students graduate from high school despite the fact that most have been in the United States since before schooling age and are often unaware of their status until they reach high school. They have been socialized by school and community influences to view themselves as Americans, equal to other citizens in every way. They have lived in the United States for most of their lives, and as a result, express an "American" identity with English as their dominant language.

From the beginning, the goal of the study was to gain a deeper understanding of the factors that shaped the pathway to college for undocumented Latino students. We came to know the participants in this study personally over the course of four years and interacted with them in various settings, including community meetings and school events. We listened to their stories of struggle and carefully observed their efforts to make better lives for themselves and their families. We also spent time with teachers, counselors, community members, university faculty and staff, and elected officials trying to understand the broader contexts of the worlds they inhabit and the relationships from which they derive support and assistance.

This fieldwork gave us the opportunity to compare what interview and survey respondents told us about their families and school experiences with what we could see from day-to-day interactions. This kind of triangulation allowed us to move beyond the role of mere observer and recorder of their stories, to be actively engaged in an investigation of the intersections of the law, community institutions, schools, and their lives. This gave us the opportunity to develop a "thick description" of the ways in which their lives are shaped by broader structures and contexts, and how they in turn, actively influence that larger world (Geertz, 1973).

Survey and in-depth interview data collection occurred over an eight-month period. Participants were recruited via e-mail and flyer advertisements to various student organizations across the country as well as on high school and college campuses. At the completion of their participation, students were asked to share the recruitment flyers with other undocumented students they knew personally. The recruitment flyers and emails invited students to participate in a research study that focused on "the educational experiences of undocumented students." This is the only detail that participants initially received regarding the purpose of the study. Email and printed flyer announcements contained a link to an online survey.

The online survey included measures of academic achievement, civic engagement, extracurricular participation, leadership positions, and enrollment in advanced level academic courses. It also consisted of school background and demographic information along with various scales designed to assess distress, bilingualism, student valuing of school, parental valuing of school, and friends valuing of school. The survey did not collect names, emails, school names, or any other type of identifying information in order to protect the identity of participants.

The third component of the study consisted of in-depth, semi-structured interviews. An advantage of the interview process is that it allows subjects to put forth personal explanations for their behavior rather than requiring them to choose among prepackaged responses. A team of trained researchers, including the authors, conducted all interviews. The team consisted of four immigrant bilingual (Spanish, English) Latino interviewers; two male and two female. All interviewers had graduate and undergraduate training in psychology and several years of social science research experience. Interviewers were trained by conducting several practice interviews that were reviewed and analyzed by the principal investigator who has extensive experience in qualitative in-depth and focus group interview methods. The investigator developed the questions according to the literature on achievement motivation and school engagement (Hodgkinson, Weitzman, 1997; Nolin, Chaney, Chapman, Chandler, 1997; Youniss, McClellan, Mazer, 2001). The initial set of questions was developed by conducting several pilot-test interviews. At the conclusion of the testing phase, the final set of interview questions was selected.

Interview participants contacted the researchers by email or phone after completing their online survey to schedule the interview. The interviews were conducted in various places including college and university campuses, coffee shops, and some by telephone. In the interview, students were asked to reflect on their social and educational experiences beginning in elementary school up to college in order to shed light on the types of challenges they encountered due to their undocumented status. The first part of the interview focused on the educational history of the students. They were asked to describe in as much detail as possible their experiences in elementary school, middle school, high school, and college when applicable. More specifically, students were asked to list and describe all academic and extracurricular participation and awards. The second part of the interviewed focused on the social, psychological, educational, and legal challenges of being undocumented. The concluding section of the interview asked students to describe their attitudes about schooling and education as well as their aspirations and ambitions for their future. All interviews were recorded, fully transcribed, and coded for analysis. After the interviews were transcribed, all audio files were permanently deleted to protect the identity of the participants.

Community College Personnel Interviews

In addition to student survey and interview data, eight interviews were conducted with community college personnel to gain an institutional perspective on the experiences of community college undocumented students. Participants consisted of a wide array of college representatives from various position levels. Most interviewees were recommended by college representatives who perceived these individuals to be knowledgeable of undocumented students. We used field notes as well as these recommendations to identify participants (Gall et al., 2003). In-depth interviews were conducted using a semi-structured interview protocol. All interviews were recorded, transcribed, and analyzed. Field notes were also analyzed consistently throughout data collection and analyses.

Student and community college personnel transcripts were read numerous times and coded for emerging themes. A process of open coding was used to generate themes (Strauss & Corbin, 1990). Procedures used to code data were systematic, including safeguards against bias and attention to descriptive, interpretive, theoretical, and evaluative validity and generalizability. The coding employed reliability checks and tests of internal and external validity (MacQueen, McLellan, Kay, & Millstein, 1998; Miles & Huberman, 1994). Independent raters first read through each interview and created narrative summaries that condensed the interview material while retaining the essence of the interviewee's stories. Each narrative summary was read independently by the data analysts who looked for themes in the summaries. A theme retained for further analysis had to be identified as a theme by at least two raters, independently. Together the qualitative and quantitative data provide both a deeper and broader perspective on the experiences of undocumented students.

Undocumented Latino Community College Students

Although the initial study included a sample of 187 undocumented high school, community college, university, college graduate, and formerly undocumented young adults from across the United States, the analyses presented here only focused on the 37 community college undocumented Latino students who participated in the study. A socioecological framework was used to understand the nuances that directly or indirectly impacted students' socioemotional well-being (Bronfenbrenner, 1979), such as family, peer, and local community members which are extremely important elements for understanding an individual's socioemotional development (Conye and Cook, 2004). Community college student transcripts were analyzed and coded for self-reported perceived self-efficacy, distress levels, perceived discrimination and rejection, educational achievements and aspirations, and support networks to determine the extent to which undocumented students experienced socioemotional difficulties. Signs of particular emotions (e.g., anxiety, despair, depression, fear, joy), internal dispositions (e.g., hope, optimism, motivation, pessimism) in relation to undocumented status were carefully noted in the analysis. Student transcripts were also coded by specific protective factors and resiliency characteristics, for example, educational achievements, coping mechanisms, and social support mechanisms. The second step was to carefully pinpoint recurrent themes throughout the 24 transcripts (Wolcott, 1990; Maxwell, 2005). Gender differences were examined to determine whether undocumented Latino males and females experience minority and legal status issues in relatively different ways.

Overall, 73% resided in California, 8% in Texas, 5% in Virginia while the remaining 13% resided in Georgia, Missouri, New York, Washington, and Washington, DC. In terms of country of origin, 88% were born in Mexico, 6% were born in Central America, while the remaining 6% were born in South America. The average age of participants was 20.5 years. Sixty percent of participants were female. The male to female ratio in the college group in this study is similar to the 61% female college enrollment rates reported for Latinos in previous studies, including the 63% female ratio reported for Mexican students (Hurtado, Saenz, Santos, and Cabrera, 2008).

Table 2.1 indicates that students, on average, arrived in the United States at 7.03 years old. As a result of their early arrival age, 100% of participants reported speaking, reading, writing, and understanding English either "well," or "very well." There was also a very high level of bilingualism among respondents with 94% reporting speaking, reading, writing, and understanding Spanish either "well," or "very well."

Table 2.1 also indicates that students grew up in homes where the parents had low levels of education. Participant mothers had about a eight years of schooling ($M = 8.15$) while fathers had about nine years of schooling ($M = 9.29$). Eighty-five percent of mothers and 74% of fathers had less than a high school education with only 6% of mothers and 16% of fathers having the equivalent of a university degree. Respondents also reported that both their mothers and fathers had low levels of English language proficiency. Only 12% of mothers and 25% of fathers spoke English either "well," or "very well." Most students did enjoy the support of both parents at home with 69% of students growing up with both parents. On average, participants had 3.24 siblings with almost 66% having three or more siblings.

Although students reported having to help in household tasks like taking care of younger siblings and doing chores, only 12% reported having to do so either "almost every day," or "once or twice a week." They did, however, report working a high number of hours per week at a job during high school. On average, students worked 15.19 hours per week. Fifty-seven percent of participants reported working 20 hours or more per week, including 11% who reported working 30 hours or more per week during high school. In college the average number of hours worked per week increased significantly to 30.52. The average was slightly higher for male students at 35.43 hours per week compared to female participants who reported working 26.89 hours per week. Overall, 70% of students reported working 20 hours or more per week during college, including 54% who reported working 30 hours or more per week.

Measures

The survey used in the original study was composed of various items that examined the socioemotional and academic support of the undocumented student (see Appendix A). Following is a brief description of the measures used.

Academic Self-Concept. The Academic Self-Efficacy scale is a 2-item scale designed to measure the participant's self-concept and predisposition as it relates to school. For example, the participants were asked to assess how much school defines who they are (e.g., "Being good in school is an important part of who I am.") or assess how important it is to be successful academically (e.g., "Doing well on intellectual tasks is very important to me."). Participants answered each item on a 7-point scale ranging from 1 (strong disagree) to 7 (strongly agree). Cronbach's alpha was 0.87, indicating strong internal reliability.

Academic Self-Efficacy. This 5-item scale measures the academic self-efficacy of each participant. Using a 5-point Likert scale, participants were asked to assess their abilities when dealing with academic challenges (e.g., "I'm certain I can master the skills taught in class this year" or "I'm certain I can figure out how to do the most difficult class work."). Items ranged from 1 (strongly disagree) to 5 (strongly agree). Cronbach's alpha was .88.

Depression. This 12-item depression scale was designed to measure the participants' sense of emotion as it relates to their legal status. More specifically, the items focused on the participant's sense of sadness (e.g., "Lately, do you feel sad"), perceptions of empathy (e.g., "Lately, do you feel others do not understand you?), or feelings like the urge to cry (e.g., "Lately, do you cry easily?"). Participants were asked to rate their emotional state on a 4-point Likert scale ranging from 1 (Never) to 4 (All the time). Cronbach's alpha was 0.87.

Discrimination. This 8-item discrimination scale was designed to measure the participant's level of exposure to discrimination as it relates to their race, ethnicity, and immigration status. The scale examined situations such as treatment by others (e.g., "Over your lifetime, how frequently have you felt treated as if you were 'stupid,' or were 'talked down to' because of your race or ethnicity?") or harassment (e.g., "Over your lifetime, how frequently have you felt insulted, been called a name, or harassed because of your race or ethnicity?"). The items were scored on a 6-point scale ranging from 1 (None) to 6 (Once a week or more). Cronbach's alpha was 0.91.

Effort Avoidance. This scale was designed to measure the participant's level of effort avoidance. More specifically, on a 2-point Likert scale, participants rated how much they avoided new and challenging academic material (e.g., "I prefer to do work as I have always done it, rather than try something new."). Each item ranged from 1(Strongly Disagree) to 5 (Strongly Agree). Cronbach's alpha for was 0.73—a moderately strong indication of reliability.

Parent-based Motivation. This 2-item scale was intended to measure how much motivation was derived from parental sacrifices and

Table 2.1 Participant Background Information

	Scale items	Alpha	%	M
Demographic				
Immigration Age<7			56	7.03
Mother's Education [a]			85	8.15
Father's Education [a]			74	9.29
Grew up with both parents			69	
Non-academic commitments				
Household responsibilities [b]			50	2.77
High School Hours worked/week [c]			57	15.19
College Hours worked/week [c]			70	30.52
Psychosocial				
Distress [g]	12	.87	3	1.99
Discrimination [h]	8	.91	0	3.06
Rejection due to Status [i]	3	.85	15	4.49
English proficiency [k]			100	3.69
Spanish proficiency [k]			94	3.57
Academic self-concept [m]	2	.87	71	6.22
Academic self-efficacy [m]	5	.88	73	6.01
Valuing of Schooling [n]	2	.82	79	6.16
Effort Avoidance [m]	2	.73	0	2.46
Parent-derived motivation [p]	2	.67	100	3.66
Parents valuing of schooling [q]	2	.83	85	3.28

N=37

[a] Percentage reflects the proportion of those with 12 years of schooling or less

[b] Scale Range: 1-5. Percent reflects responses 4-5 combined.

[c] Percent reflects the proportion of those working more than 20 hrs/wk.

[g] Scale Range: 1-4. Percent reflects responses 3-4 combined.

[h] Scale Range: 1-6. Percent reflects responses 5-6 combined.

[i] Scale Range: 1-7. Percent reflects responses 6-7 combined.

[k] Scale Range: 1-4. Percent reflects responses 3-4 combined.

[m] Scale Range: 1-7. Percent reflects responses 6-7 combined.

[n] Scale Range: 1-7. Percent reflects responses 6-7 combined.

[p] Scale Range: 1-4. Percent reflects responses 3-4 combined.

[q] Scale Range: 1-4. Percent reflects responses 3-4 combined.

economic stability. The sample items included "I want to do well in school to make my parents happy" and "Because I want to help my family have a better life." The response options ranged from 1 (Very true) to 4 (Very false). Notably, variables were actually scored in a reversed direction when compared to the other variables in the original survey. Cronbach's alpha was .67.

Parental Valuing of Schooling. This 2-item scale is designed to assess how much the participants' parents encourages them to perform well academically. This sample included the following: "For my parents, my getting good grades in school is very important" and "For my parents, my going to college after high school is very important." The response options ranged from 1 (Not important) to 4 (Very important). Cronbach's alpha was 0.83.

Rejection Due to Legal Status. This 3-item scale measured the level of rejection a participant feels as it related to their undocumented status. Using a Likert-scale range of 1 (Never) to 7(Always), participants assessed their perceptions of the following sample questions: "Because of my AB540 background, I feel that I am not wanted in this country" or "Because of my AB540 background, I don't feel accepted by other Americans." Cronbach's alpha was .85.

Valuing of School. This scale provided a measure of how much each participant valued his or her education. As undocumented students, it was important to assess their level of enthusiasm and commitment to achieving a post-secondary education considering their systematic limitations. Using a 2-item Likert-scale, participants answered each item (e.g., How important is it to you to earn good grades in college?) using a range of 1 (Not at all) to 7 (Very important). Cronbach's alpha was 0.82.

Student In-depth Interview Sample

Twenty-four survey participants also agreed to be interviewed. The background characteristics of interview participants did not vary much from the survey sample. Eighty-five percent originally emigrated from Mexico, 10% from South America, and 4% were from Central America. The average age for interview participants was 21.7 while 87% were female. Table 2.2 indicates that these participants had lived in the United States about 18 years, and had immigrated to the U.S.

before schooling age, similar to the overall survey sample. Seventy-four of respondents came from two-parent households. The average level of education for interview respondents' mothers was about 8.09 years of schooling, while for fathers it was about 9.16 years. Participants reported that their parents' employment was mostly in blue-collar jobs (e.g, food service, housekeeping, construction, garment factories, and warehouses).

Table 2.2 Interview Participant Demographic Information

Pseudonym	Gender	Age	Yrs. in U.S.	Mother's Years of School	Father's Years of School	Lives with Both Parents	GPA
Carla	Female	23	19	4	5	Yes	2.70
Daniela	Female	19	N/A	2	N/A	Yes	3.30
Guillermo	Male	28	21	N/A	N/A	Yes	3.80
Isabel	Female	21	19	14	8	Yes	3.30
Jacinto	Male	22	19	8	12	No	3.30
Jack	Male	20	16	3	3	Yes	N/A
Jacqueline	Female	19	18	12	6	Yes	4.00
Jazmin	Female	20	20	16	16	Yes	2.90
Jimena	Female	21	17	6	11	No	3.15
Jocelin	Female	21	14	5	12	No	3.20
Karen	Female	18	N/A	12	N/A	No	3.79
Linda	Female	20	12	8	6	Yes	3.34
Liz	Female	24	18	6	N/A	No	3.40
Lucila	Female	18	19	6	15	Yes	N/A
Lucy	Female	22	7	3	6	Yes	3.50
Michelle	Female	23	18	10	12	Yes	3.70
Miriam	Female	21	19	12	8	Yes	2.80
Monica	Female	21	17	7	9	Yes	3.70
Olivia	Female	22	10	16	16	No	2.60
Paulina	Female	34	27	2	3	Yes	3.60
Rosa	Female	26	N/A	4	4	Yes	2.00
Sasha	Female	19	14	17	16	Yes	3.80
Thalia	Female	19	17	5	6	Yes	3.20

Note: N/A denotes missing data

Overall, the students in this study arrived in the United States before schooling age, are highly bilingual, and grew up in homes with low levels of parental education and parental English proficiency. The next chapter examines the challenges that community college undocumented students face growing up and after they graduate from high school in their pursuit of higher education

CHAPTER 3

Arriving at the Higher Education Gateway: Challenges and Barriers

Although many undocumented community college students in the study more than exceed the criteria for admission into four-year colleges and universities, the affordability of community colleges provides students with the only viable path to a college degree. Many are initially admitted to top four-year schools, but were forced to decline due to financial constraints (Chavez et al., 2007; Oliverez, 2006). Community colleges bring down costs by allowing students to enroll full-time or half-time at lower fees (Dozier, 2001; Jauregui et al., 2008; Oliverez, 2006). Among students surveyed in our study, eighty-percent (80%) reported planning to transfer to a four-year institution upon completing their general education requirements. Even though community colleges provide an opportunity to undocumented students where few exist, students face a variety of challenges and frustrations because community colleges are ill-prepared to serve a student population they hardly understand, and often times, are hardly aware of their presence on campus. Faced with few or no other alternatives, the community college system becomes the primary entry point to higher education for most undocumented students. This chapter provides an in-depth examination of the social and educational experiences of undocumented Latino community college students, including the primary obstacles they face in their pursuit of a college education.

The Border-crossing Experience

For many of the participants, their lives changed dramatically when their parents made the decision to bring them to the United States. Students like Guillermo were uprooted from their homelands by their parents in order to seek financial stability and safety in the U.S:

> I came to the United States in 1986 when I was 7 years old. In El Salvador, I was born in a rural area, where I lived till the age of 1 1/2. At that point, the civil war in El Salvador had gotten pretty intense...We literally had to leave with whatever we had on our backs.

Guillermo's parents left for the United States to find work and housing, but due to the high risks and cost of crossing the U.S. border, Guillermo and his younger brother stayed behind with their grandmother until his parents had saved enough money to send for them. As the civil war escalated, Guillermo was at risk of being drafted by both the Salvadoran National Army and the Farabundo Marti National Liberation Front (FMLN) leftist guerilla army. His parents had to expedite the process of bringing both of their children to the United States. Guillermo recalled that the journey was a traumatic experience for him and his younger brother:

> Crossing the border wasn't easy. We actually got detained at the border, when we were trying to cross...I remember being in the back of a pickup truck and trying to cross the border, and all of a sudden the pickup truck gets stopped and they open up the back and I see men in uniform motioning us to get out. I didn't know exactly what was going on...Then my little brother, who was 6 years old at the time, they took him and he was crying... I thought maybe they were going to do something to us...I remember snapshots of being in a detention center for about 2 weeks. We were first placed in this huge hall with bunk beds, and it was just my dad and my brother and me, and then another man, with his two sons...Later we got placed into a cell just with my father and my brother. I remember my dad complaining that this wasn't

Arriving at the Higher Education Gateway: Challenges & Barriers 47

an appropriate place for him and his family because right next to our bed was the toilet.

For students like Guillermo, their feelings of being unwanted initially began when they arrived at the border.

Other participants did not have to risk their lives to cross the U.S./Mexican border. As children, some participants arrived in the U.S. with tourist visas. In fact, several of the participants didn't realize that they would be staying permanently. For example, Lucy, who was 15 years old when she learned she was undocumented, expressed how distraught she became when she learned she would be staying in the U.S.:

> We were told that we were going to come [to the U.S.] for one month or so, just for a vacation, but... my aunt, she started talking to my parents about staying, "Now that you're here, why do you want to go back? You have the opportunity to come without risking your life..." they decided to stay then...I didn't like that. I was just crying and asking my parents...begging my father especially to let me go back...but he said, "No, this is going to be fine. You're going to learn English. You need to learn English and you need to continue on with your education here. Look at your cousins. Look at your aunt, they speak perfect English and you can also speak the language that they are speaking," so I had no option.

Although Guillermo and Lucy had different journeys to the U.S., what most of the students in this study had in common was the socioeconomic distress in their country of origin that led to their parents' decision to immigrate. In fact, all 24 participants shared that their parents had expressed to them at some point while they were growing up that they decide to come to the U.S. to provide them with a better future.

Attitudes Toward Parents

Three of the 24 students outwardly expressed feelings of resentment toward their parents for bringing them without legal authorization to the United States. Daniela, a second-year community college student, stated that at times she did not know how to deal with the discrimination and frustrations of being undocumented, and in turn, blamed her parents for her anguish:

> As far as with my parents, I was going through problems with them just because I would blame them a lot for my situation, for being an undocumented student...like I tried to apply for certain things and I was rejected. So those things kind of didn't help, and I know it was not the right thing, but I blamed my parents for bringing me here, and I wasn't very happy.

Isabel did not learn that she was undocumented until she was 13 years old, an age that she looked forward to because she thought she would be able to get a part-time job:

> I remember that I was looking forward to being 13, because when you're 13 you can go to work. I'm thinking, "OK, that's the first job I'm going to get." Then, I remember, this guy was like, "Oh, we'll help you fill out the application." Then I see the letters, "SS," and I'm like, "What's SS?" They're like, "Oh, social security number." "What's that?" They say, "Oh, I'm sure you have one. Just ask your mom." I went home and I asked my mom, "Mom, what's a social security?" She says, "Oh, well, it's this number that they give to citizens." And I'm like, "Do I have one?" She's like, "No, you don't." I'm like, "So that means I can't work?" She says, "No, I'm afraid not." And I'm like, "Oh, OK." And it didn't hit me back then how serious that would end up being later on.

It was usually through a situation like the one Isabel described that undocumented students first began to realize their fate as adults. Oftentimes, their parents were afraid to share such information because they feared their child might be detained by immigration officials if they inadvertently disclosed their status to school personnel or strangers. Like Daniela and Isabel, some students felt betrayed by their parents, especially when they were not told until it was time to apply for college.

Arriving at the Higher Education Gateway: Challenges & Barriers 49

Attitudes Toward Peers

Once students realized that they were not legal residents, they became more aware of their limited opportunities such as the inability to qualify for federal and state funded college preparation programs and financial aid, scholarships, study abroad programs, and employment. Estrella, a third-year community college student, described her moments of anger and resentment when she compared her options to those of her peers:

> There are a lot of students that don't take advantage of what they have. I get mad, and I got a little bit upset, like two months ago...I was even crying in front of my mom...I was talking to her in Spanish and I told her that I get so mad that there are friends who are citizens or legal and don't even want to go to college.

Jimena also felt resentment towards some of her American peers who did not take advantage of the opportunities she wished she had:

> Now that I think about it, most of my friends who are legal, they didn't continue with their education. Most of them are either married or they have kids. Or they're working a regular job that doesn't pay well. That gets me angry because there are so many things that they can do. They can get scholarships and funding to do things. They just don't want to do it. I want to do it, but I can't.

Lucila echoed the same sentiments when asked about her perceptions about how American citizens view undocumented students:

> I've listened to the ones who think that we're stealing their children's education, but I mean, come on, how are we stealing their education when most get a full financial aid package, but they don't even want to take advantage of the resources. It's like things are handed to them, they just don't want to take it and yet we're struggling back here trying to find a way to survive.

Overall, 7 of the 24 interview participants expressed their rancor toward their U.S. born peers who they felt chose to not take advantage of the opportunities that college-going undocumented students need but are not able to access.

Shame, Fear, and Anxiety

Along with fear and aggravation, others develop feelings of shame. For example, Jacinto, a second-year community college student, expressed the following:

> It shouldn't be, but it's more like I'm ashamed. I'm not like everyone else...I don't have an ID, and I don't have a driver's license. If someone asked for an ID, I have to take out a passport, and especially now with all the immigration debates, I really don't want to speak out.

Jacinto often feels a sense of humiliation and voicelessness due to his undocumented status. In addition to shame, students also expressed a generalized sense of fear and depression as Esperanza described:

> I get scared of applying for scholarships. I still haven't done my internship in broadcasting because I'm scared that whenever I get to go to a radio station, they might ask me for a social security card; and that I won't be able to get a job if I get to get my degree...I do get depressed and I get disappointed that, you know, I am doing all this work; and for me to graduate and not be able to work in the field that I want... instead I have to get another job instead of a job I love.

Similarly, the hardest thing for Paulina is always feeling afraid:

> I think I am always afraid...it's like, I am walking down the street or wherever I am, and I am completely aware of myself, to make sure that I am not doing anything I am not supposed to...being responsible for everything that I do. Making sure I am not doing anything at all. And I'm just afraid. I am afraid.

Carla also described her sense of uncertainty:

> The uncertainty that you have...like the way you look at your future, you kind of want to stick to looking at things moment-by-moment, because if you look really far beyond, sometimes it gets you depressed...I don't know what's going to happen.

Sasha, a second-year community college student, constantly worries about a future as an unemployable college graduate:

> It's hard because I know that at one point I am going to graduate; and even though I have a college degree, what am I going to do with it if nobody wants to hire me? It's been very difficult. It is difficult because I feel like I have the capacity to contribute to the economy but I can't be considered. That's very difficult because I have a drive to do better and to work hard to contribute, but I just don't have the means to do it.

Jimena lamented being forced to put herself in a precarious legal situation just to get to school and feeling embarrassed when she is out socializing with friends:

> It's difficult, even with little things like driving. I have to drive illegally, whether I want to or not. Every time that I see a cop, I get really nervous that he's going to pull me over...Also, little things like going to a dance club, where they require you to show your I.D. I've actually been rejected from a lot of clubs because they told me that I needed to be 21. I tell them that I am, and I show them my Mexican I.D., but they tell me that it isn't a California I.D. and that it doesn't show my height or weight. It's embarrassing because you have a bunch of your friends around you and you can't get in.

Esperanza, Irene, Carla, Paulina, and Jimena's comments reflect the typical concerns, experiences, and emotions experienced by the undocumented community college students we interviewed. The dehumanizing episodes these students generally experience and the overwhelming sense of rejection and fear of deportation often create a great sense of insecurity. Fulfilling simple needs such as driving a car or enjoying a night of fun become major problems which result in high levels of fear and anxiety. These recurring experiences and the uncertainty about their futures often lead to despair and depression.

Anti-immigrant Sentiment

Along with having to overcome various legal and institutional barriers, participants learned from an early age about the pervasive anti-immigrant sentiment. Approximately 16 of the 23 participants reported experiencing prejudice and microaggressions (Solarzano, Ceja, & Yosso, 2000) in their schools, communities, and the media. Like Esperanza, various participants reported both positive and negative experiences:

> I would say that there is a percentage that likes us, and they do appreciate whatever we are trying to do. They tell us to fight back; but there's also a greater, a much greater percentage that just doesn't want us here...they think that we're taking away things from them, which we're not.

Daniela also shared Esperanza's view that there are those that are supportive and understanding and others that are not:
> Well, there's good and bad everywhere, so I feel that there are people who sympathize with us, who do understand...I mean, we're not here because we chose to be here and...we don't go back because we can't go back; but there are people who honestly don't understand why we're here, don't understand why we were brought here, and really don't understand what we go through.

Valerie also described both positive and negative encounters:

> I've been very lucky in that respect because I've always encountered people that are Caucasian and don't really care about my status. It doesn't matter to them whether I'm legal or not. But there are also people I know from past experiences who just think less of you. They think that you don't have what it takes to accomplish things, and they think that we're

just here to be on welfare and child support, and things like that. They think that we take their money and their jobs.

Jack also described the public misconception that he and others like him are a drain on social services:

> Some people see us as straining the system or doing more harm than good, and I think that is too bad of them to think this way...we should have the opportunity to improve ourselves. We help the United States to become what it is: A Great Nation.

Linda lamented feeling devalued and the public apathy about the plight of undocumented students:

> They don't think we're that important...If we could do something with our education, they're just fine. If we can just pay for it and go to college, I think it's just fine with them, but they don't want to take that extra step to try to help us, or anything. If we're there, that's fine. They're not going to put us out of the school, but they're not going to do anything for us, either.

Irene described her frustration with pervasive negative images about undocumented immigrations:

> We're not like criminals, we're not trying to steal anything from anybody. It's just that we want to continue the dream that our parents started when they brought us here for a better future...it's hard because it's like you find people that will put you down, and you're like, "OK, should I continue? Is this going to get harder, or this is going to get better?"

Irene also expressed frustration about the lack of public awareness into the various factors that force individuals to leave their country of origin and migrate:

> I think they view us as aliens, and they view us like we are criminals, like we shouldn't even be helped at all, like the [California] law AB540 should have not even passed. "Why should we help those people who came here illegally, who didn't even bother to file an application to enter here legally?" I feel that they don't think, or they don't really see what motivates immigration here, what brings us here. For example, I see some people that say, "Oh, then why are you here, if you don't want to be called an immigrant, if you don't want to be called illegal?" It's like, "Hello, I didn't choose to come here. I was 8 years old. How is an 8-year-old going to say to her parents, 'No, I can't go. I don't want to go.' If I stayed there, who was I going to stay with?"

Most students described anti-immigrant sentiments as a central theme in their lives. They often have to deal with public ignorance and apathy on a regular basis. Feeling unwelcome, and perceived as "criminals" by American society is a common experience for undocumented students.

Discrimination

Inevitably, experiencing discrimination has become a familiar pattern for undocumented Latino students. They carry the burden of a "triple minority status" in that they're a target for discrimination based on their ethnic background, lack of legal status, and economic disadvantages, all of which pose great socioemotional distress. Like other undocumented Latino community college students, Jacinto often felt devalued in his interaction with others:

> Sometimes you get the feeling that people are talking down to you. In the service industry, people, just in general, they look at you. I don't think it's just myself, I think it's any person who is a minority that is looked down upon. They don't really give you a chance sometimes.

Thalia added, "You go to a place where it is mostly white people. They make faces at you; they give you dirty looks. They give you looks like

Arriving at the Higher Education Gateway: Challenges & Barriers 55

you are a kind of monster." Monica reported experiencing racial profiling:

> I experience discrimination just walking down the street or going to the supermarket. If I am in an area where it is primarily Caucasian, I am still being followed. I mean, unfortunately, it just doesn't stop. You learn to fight your battles.

Classmates and other peers were often the perpetrators of discriminatory behavior as Miriam explained:

> In high school, there was a lot of discrimination from some of my peers because I was Mexican and had a strong accent. These students knew that I was in an ESL program. It's like you're stupid to them. So this experience kind of made me gravitate towards minorities instead of trying to hang out with students who were not.

As she got older, Lucia experienced increasing discrimination and feelings of rejection:

> I think even as an adult, it's still difficult because you're being rejected from a public place where you think everybody should be entitled to go, like a restaurant…I feel like there's been a backlash with all the immigration things…in the past 3 years I've experienced it more than ever before in my whole life…I just experienced it 2 weeks ago when we tried to go to Universal City and get into a restaurant. They wouldn't let me in, and the guy made very sure that he said, "I'm sorry man, I can let everybody in, but she's not welcome here." And so I said, "What do you mean by not welcome?" He said, "I'm sorry, I don't want to talk to you. You can't come into my restaurant."

Several students reported being denied entry into various establishments (e.g., restaurants or night clubs) simply because they did not have state-issued identification. In Lucia's case, foreign consulate-issued identification cards (e.g., *matricula consular*) often triggered suspicions of illegal status. In addition to exclusion due to their legal status, undocumented students also experience discrimination based on their ethnic background, English proficiency, and socioeconomic background. Participants felt that others viewed them as "social outcasts or inferior."

Gender Discrimination

For Daniela and other female participants, they not only had to struggle with discrimination based on their undocumented and minority statuses, but they also had to deal with gender discrimination:

> being born a Latina woman and with a dark-skinned complexion... I don't have a light complexion...there are people who discriminate against that. I feel that I have been discriminated against—I always have to prove that as a woman I could also do the things that anybody else can do.

A stereotype that female participants reported was the widespread perception of young Latina women as teen parents. Sasha explained, "To this day, I always get the rudest question of all: 'How many kids do you have?' When I say, 'Oh I don't have any children,' they're shocked: 'Why don't you have any children?' they ask." Sasha, who was only 19 years of age, was disturbed and frustrated to hear such comments regularly. This was a common sentiment for many of the female participants.

When asked to rate their feelings of marginalization due to their undocumented status, 15% reported feeling that way, either, "always," "almost always," or "often." According to Table 3.1, on average, students felt rejected due to their status somewhere between "sometimes," and "often" (M=4.49). However, when asked about lifetime experiences with overt prejudice and discrimination, on average, students reported experiencing discrimination, "a few times," ($M = 3.06$). Overall, students also reported low levels of psychological distress with only 3% reporting feeling stressed either, "often," or "all the time." Perhaps reflecting the immigrant optimism that has been documented in previous research (Suarez-Orozco, 1989; Suarez-Orozco

& Suarez-Orozco, 1995) few reported specific incidents with prejudice and discrimination. Along the same lines, students report low levels of distress despite their legal marginality.

The Community College Experience

For undocumented students, the relative affordability of the community college often provides the only path to higher education. Regardless of their academic accomplishments, students like Daniela are generally excluded from four-year universities because they cannot afford the tuition:

> I felt that going to community college would just give me a little bit more time to just raise more money, to find more resources, and hopefully by the time I graduated from community college I would have saved some money to pay for the university.

Table 3.1 Psychosocial Distress

	%	M
Psychosocial Measures		
Distress [a]	3	1.99
Discrimination [b]	0	3.06
Rejection due to Status [c]	15	4.49

N=37

[a] Scale range: 1 *(never)* - 4 *(all the time)*. Percent reflects responses 3-4 combined.
[b] Scale range: 1 *(never)* - 6 *(always)*. Percent reflects responses 5-6 combined.
[c] Scale range: 1 *(never)* - 7 *(always)*. Percent reflects responses 6-7 combined.

Some community colleges provided financial assistance to undocumented students in the form of small scholarships. For students attending school in states where they were allowed to pay resident in-state tuition fees, as opposed to the international student fees they would otherwise have had to pay, the lower tuition rate was a significant form of financial support as Jacinto describes, "I got a scholarship here for $200 just because of my high GPA, so they do help out a little. The waiver that we don't have to pay international tuition is a great help. It makes it possible for us to attend."

One of the most salient themes for community college students was the difficulty balancing school with other obligations and responsibilities. Students like Beatriz were constantly concerned about not being able to pay for their tuition or apply to the school of their choice due to cost:

> When I was in high school I had applied to a private school, but being undocumented, and it's so expensive, I couldn't get scholarships or financial aid, and I didn't want my dad to be paying $60,000 for something that I may not like. So I decided that it was just too expensive so I decided to go to a community college and this is where I am. It has been a long 4 years because stuff happens. Like with money, or you have to go to work, somehow it delays itself, but I am going to finish hopefully in one year. Now I am taking a year off of school to work and save up.

Beatriz was working forty hours per week at the time of the interview. Nailea, a second year student, had also experienced difficulties paying for her college expenses. Like Beatriz, she has also had to take time off from school, "It's been rough. I have been having to pay everything on my own. I have had to take off a couple of quarters because of no money."

Work & Financial Hardships

One of the main difficulties undocumented students face is finding ways to pay for their college tuition and other related expenses. Because most do not qualify for federal and state financial aid, the only way to cope with this problem is to work as many hours possible, to cover both school and personal expenses. In high school, most participants worked an average of 20 hours per week ($M = 19.69$, $SD = 6.63$), and in college it increased to nearly full-time status at an average of 32 hours per week (M = 32.42, SD = 18.47). Lucia describes how she had to learn how to balance multiple jobs and school:

> I had to hustle... I would clean houses, I would take care of people's kids, I would mow lawns, I would do anything just to make sure I got that money to pay for the classes every quarter. I would sign up for them, and then when the bill came in past due...I figured, even if they kick me out of the class by the third week...because I didn't pay the bill...I still got the knowledge in the first three weeks, you know, so I didn't care.

For Liliana, it was difficult to work, do well in her classes and get involved in extracurricular activities, "It's been hard [working full-time and attending school full-time] because I really can't focus too much on my homework, and again, I really can't do any other activities after classes because I'm always working." Estrella constantly worried about school costs and helping her family financially:

> That's why I have to work, so we can have some more money for the books. I don't know how much the books are going to cost, and I have to save money also to buy some other stuff, and to pay some debts that we have.

One of the hardest things for Dulce was not being able to get scholarships that she earned due to her academic accomplishments:

> I was offered the Presidential Scholarship at Cal State Long Beach, but when they learned of my status, they said I couldn't get it...I could have gone to school for free, and that would have been the difference.

Instead of attending school on a full scholarship, Dulce also had to work long hours while going to school, "My first three years, I had to work as an office manager and invoice transcriber, and it was hard having to study and work 40 hours a week." Although many students received some financial assistance from their parents, it was often not enough to cover all of the costs. Sasha, echoed Dulce's sentiments, "As an undocumented student, it has been difficult just because in terms of the economic aspect, there's not a lot of support. It's hard to pay for school." Esperanza worried about the rising cost of school and the various friends that have dropped out because they can no longer afford to pay their tuition:

> When I started going to school...the units were $11, so I was happy, but when they got to $18, I was like, "Oh, my God, what am I going to do now? Am I going to work more or am I going to stop going? Like what am I going to do? I can afford $11, anybody can afford that, but $18, and then it went up to $26. When it got to $18, a lot of my classmates that are undocumented dropped out. They stopped attending, they started working, and I would be like, "When are you going back to school?" They're like, "Oh, I need to save money," and it's bad because they haven't come back and I'm afraid that they're not going to do it anymore.

Sasha's, Dulce's, and Esperanza's worries were a common experience for all participants. Many expressed their frustration and their overwhelming feeling of uncertainty. Further contributing to the emotional setbacks were the countless opportunities and scholarships that require proof of legal status. Unfortunately, many students were left to seek other alternatives in their pursuit of higher education.

Institutional Challenges

In addition to financial concerns, and balancing work with school, undocumented students at the community college also face a variety of institutional challenges. Daniela spent a lot of time researching the school she attended because many of the schools she visited did not support undocumented students, "I went to other colleges and I tried to find out what they offer for undocumented students and a lot of schools didn't even know what that meant. They had very little information and I just felt very disappointed." Isabel also describes a lack of support for undocumented students at her community college, "I don't think they do as much as they probably could do. You're on your own. If there was a way of getting maybe the word out or getting some more help, that would be great."

Participants reported other types of exclusion due to their legal status. Oftentimes, school agents were the culprits of discriminatory behavior, like the counselor described by Irene:

> There was one time when I told a counselor that I was AB540. Then he goes, "Oh, what's that?" I was like, "Oh, that's..." and I started to explain. Then he goes, "Oh, does that exist?" "Like, yeah." And he's like, "Oh, but...you're an immigrant, that's what it is, right?" And I was like, "Yeah, but mainly, it's a law that was passed and it allows us." And he goes, "Oh, well, you still can't make it in life, so why do you bother?" So I was like, "Whoa!"

Dulce also experienced lack of sympathy from community college personnel:

> There was a time at the community college I attended that I needed a transcript. The clerk asked for an I.D., and I said, "Oh, OK," and I showed her my college I.D. She said, "No, you need a California I.D." I'm like, "No, I don't need a California I.D. I'm showing you an I.D. This serves the same purpose." She's like, "Well, we need a valid I.D.," so I showed her my passport and she said, "OK, well, where's your social security number?" "I don't have to have a social security number."

Community college undocumented Latino students experience a myriad of socioemotional hardships due to their minority, low-income, and undocumented status backgrounds. These emotions range from resentment toward significant others, rejection due to systemic policies, and discrimination based on cultural biases and anti-immigrant sentiment. Remarkably, though, the socioemotional functioning of these participants was quite stable in spite of all of the barriers they faced. Academically, these students suffered from limited resources, and often had to work twice as hard to accomplish their educational and career goals. In fact, many of the participants worked extremely long hours to pay for their educational and personal expenses. In addition, female participants were more likely to be burdened with extra layers of gender biases.

Community college students struggled to balance their school work with their jobs. Students experienced various interruptions in their schooling because they had to take a leave from school due to a lack of funds to pay tuition. They expressed disappointment in having to stay longer at the community college because they can't remain enrolled continuously, despite their long work hours. Various students report working in excess of 40 hours per week. Students also report some institutional barriers. Some students noted that their community college had no idea who undocumented students were and had no resources in place to help them. The various forms and paperwork they have to fill out to attend and requests for their social security number or drivers license was a frequent reminder of their stigma. Students were also not able to join various academic support programs or complete required internships because they required proof of legal status or a social security number. Finally, students constantly worried about the ever increasing cost of tuition. Many described friends who dropped out and did not return because they could not afford the increasing tuition rates.

The findings raise questions about how these students cope with the adversity they face on a regular bases. Their moderate levels of depression are surprising, considering the various challenges they described. Although undocumented students experience frequent hardships they may also rely on the emotional and financial support of their families and external social support networks to buffer stressors related to their status, ethnic origin, and economic struggles (Finch et al., 2000; Finch & Vega, 2003). Male and female students may vary in their coping styles, personal characteristics, and internal dispositions. As such, the following chapter examines the factors that may play a protective role that allows them to develop and maintain high levels of optimism and motivation to achieve despite the obstacles they face.

CHAPTER 4
Coping, Social Support, And Achievement

Jauregui and Slate (2009) note wide variability in academic achievement among community college undocumented students. Whereas some were high academic achievers and more motivated to succeed than students who were U.S. citizens, others had similar academic qualities as their average high school peer graduates, including areas of general academic deficiencies. Undocumented students also arrived at the community college with varying educational backgrounds and differing levels of English proficiency, including many who had spent a significant part of their primary and secondary schooling in Mexico. In this chapter, we examined in more detail the ways in which undocumented Latino community college students cope with the challenges they encounter as well as the role of parents, institutional agents, and peers as sources of information and of social and academic support.

Academically, community college students reported an average high school GPA of 3.14 and a college GPA of 3.13. They also report taking an average of 2.14 Advanced Placement (AP) and Honors in high school and having received an average of 4.51 academic awards such as student of the month, honor roll, spelling bee, and merit-based scholarships during their schooling years. Overall, about a third (29%) reported having been identified as gifted early in their schooling and participating in Gifted and Talented Education (GATE) and magnet

Table 4.1 Student Academic Profiles

	%	Mean
Academic		
High School GPA [a]	32	3.14
College GPA [a]	29	3.13
AP/Honors courses [b]	57	2.14
Academic Awards [b]	92	4.51
GATE	29	
Extracurricular Participation	95	4.76
Psychosocial		
Dual Frame of Reference [c]	69	5.77
Orientation towards schooling		
Educational Aspirations [d]	80	5.37
Educational Expectations [d]	51	4.69
Academic self-concept [c]	71	6.22
Academic self-efficacy [c]	73	6.01
Valuing of Schooling [e]	79	6.16
Effort Avoidance [c]	68	2.46
Parent-derived motivation [f]	100	3.66
Social support for schooling		
Parents valuing of schooling [g]	85	3.28

N=37

[a] Percent represents the proportion of those with a 3.5 GPA or above

[b] Percent reporting 1 or more

[c] Scale range: 1-7. Percent reflects responses 6-7 combined.

[d] Scale range: 1 *(graduate from high school)* - 6 *(J.D./Ph.D./M.D. degree)*. Percent reflects responses 5-6 combined.

[e] Scale range: 1–7. Percent reflects responses 6-7 combined.

[f] Scale range: 1 - 4. Percent reflects responses 3-4 combined.

[g] Scale range: 1 - 4. Percent reflects responses 3-4 combined.

programs. Despite multiple challenges and various demands on their time, 95% of undocumented community college Latino students had participated in some form of extracurricular activity at least once during their schooling years. Students also reported high educational aspirations and expectations. Table 4.1 indicates that on average, students aspired to earn at least a Master's degree, but expected to only earn a B.A. degree.

Table 4.1 shows that more than two-thirds (69%) of students "strongly agree" that their conditions in the U.S. are much better than their country of origin. When asked a series of questions about whether being a good student was an important part of their self-image (Academic Self-Concept), almost three-fourths (71%) strongly agreed. Similarly, in their responses to a series of questions about whether they felt confident in their academic abilities (Academic Self-Efficacy), 73% strongly agreed. Overall, 79% reported that doing well in school is "very important" (Valuing of Schooling). Students also reported engaging in difficult academic work as noted by the 68% of respondents that "Strongly Disagree" with a series of questions asking whether they avoid academically difficult tasks (Effort-Avoidance). In response to questions that asked whether they were motivated by others to do well academically, 100% reported that it was "somewhat true" or "very true" of them to be motivated by their parents (parent-derived achievement motivation). Similarly, 85% reported that education was either "important" or "very important" for their parents (Parental Valuing of Education).

Social and Academic Support from School Agents

Important sources of support for undocumented community college students were teachers, counselors, faculty and other school agents. Beatriz's faculty advisor, for example, was one of the most influential people in her life, "She has always been there for me, I could always go up to her and tell her anything. She understands where I come from and she knows my situation." Jacqueline also found a mentor at her community college, "My mentor was very important because she was like, 'We will find a solution. Don't worry, we will find a way.' She talked to some people, asked around, always looking out for me."

Juana's history professor had a profound influence on her because he came from a similar socioeconomic background:

> My history professor is very down to earth. He's real. He grew up in the same areas that I did...I would say that he's one of the professors that really inspired me because he started from the ghetto too. He started from scratch and he worked his way up and he's working on his PhD degree...It's awesome to see that.

Approximately 21 of the 27 students reported teachers and counselors as key institutional agents that were influential and supportive figures in their academic lives. For example, despite the humiliation and rejection that Dulce experienced with the community college counselor, she still managed to overcome the adversity with the encouragement of her high school teachers and assistant principal:

> There were five teachers that encouraged me and would tell me, "Well, you can't give up now! You have to continue. There has to be a way…" Mr. C., who was the assistant principal at my high school, would call his friends and ask for funding. He would just encourage me to continue and not give up. And then there was this other teacher, Ms. S. She contacted one of her friends, and her friend gave me a scholarship, which I received all throughout my college career.

Jacinto relied on the support of his English teacher:

> She helped me a lot with my writing. She told me that I have a talent for writing. She told me to try my best to go to a university because she thought that I would really excel. Having people at the professional level that believe in you really pushes you.

Rosa also received encouragement from various teachers. She stated, "Up to this point, I have had positive influences from teachers. I've had teachers who have always helped me out…just encouraging me in different ways." Guillermo received significant support from his college counselor, one of the few people he trusted with his secret:

> I sought the advice of my college counselor, and she knew my situation. She was one of the few people at the school who knew exactly what my situation was here as an undocumented student, and she knew my potential, also. She was one of the ones that motivated me to really do well in school. And when I thought about not continuing my education, which at one point I did, very briefly, just because I thought there was nothing else that could be done, that the dream of going to college was crushed at that moment, my college counselor disagreed. She said, "There's no way you are going to stop going to school. This is what we need to do, and it's not a matter of whether you want to—it's that you're going to."

Daniela expressed her initial ambivalence about attending a predominantly white community college institution because she was accustomed to attending schools with mostly Latino students. However, her attitude changed when she met her sociology professor:

> I met a professor in a sociology course that I took and she was very inspirational, the way she taught stuff, the way she just talked about her class and lecture. I guess she was one of the people that kind of influenced me, because I was feeling culture shock when I got there.

Daniela's example highlights how student background and campus climate may have a significant impact on a undocumented students' sense of belonging or comfort. Having only attended homogeneous Latino student institutions all her life, Daniela needed extra support to help with her transition. As in Daniela's case, it was not uncommon for undocumented students to come from primarily minority-serving high schools and communities (Gándara, 2005). In some cases, some students rarely left their predominantly Latino neighborhoods, even after they started college.

Parental Support

Students also received support and encouragement from parents. Overall, 26 of the 27 participants shared positive feelings about their parents or guardians, and described the guidance and support they received from them. Isabel stated:

> They've done so much economically and spiritually. They're the ones who have given me the opportunity to attend college. Right now I am unemployed. I do some low-level work and help people out with their yards...my parents are the ones who've been helping me right now in college. They have played a significant role.

Diego explained his mother's advise to pursue educational opportunities not available to her as a child and her belief that education would pave the way to success:

> My mother always told me that school was the only way for me to succeed....She always says that I have more opportunities than her because she couldn't attend elementary school, and that we could help her...or help others in the future, once we succeed.

Monica's parents also encouraged education to ensure that she capitalize on opportunities not available to them because they were not able to receive much formal schooling:

> My parents always push me to go to school. They always encouraged us because they didn't have much education, formal education. So they knew that they had very hard and tough lives because of that. They couldn't get the jobs that they were very much capable of doing, because of that, so they always encouraged us to go to school.

Valerie also credits her parents for helping her remain committed to schooling and not to give up despite her uncertain future:

> It could've been easy for them [parents] to say, since I finished high school and I can't work in a real job or a good job, to work where they don't ask for the social security number. But no, ever since I was small they've encouraged me. And although I was going to face that obstacle, they just encourage me and tell me that I can do it. And they tell me one day there might be a solution for me. So it's definitely my parents who put me in college.

Parents encouraged their children to pursue higher education in part to avoid the hardships they endured in their physically demanding low-wage jobs due to their lack of formal education. In a scenario described by many participants, Jimena explained her mother's tactics to encourage her to continue with her education:

> I would sit down with my mom, and she would say, "Do you really want to clean bathrooms like me?" She would drag me to work on the weekends, and I hated it. She would clean houses, and they were families with kids or boys my age, and I would be very embarrassed.

Examples like Jimena's were common experiences for most participants when they growing up. Over the years, participants recounted the admiration and appreciation that they developed for their parents.

Peer Influence and Support

Peers also played an important role in helping students deal with the various challenges. In particular, older undocumented peers with more knowledge about higher education became critical supports. Irene greatly benefited from the relationships she developed with other undocumented students:

I actually know a lot of UCLA students that are undocumented, and I was amazed because I learned that ...it's possible to go to college and earn a degree and everything...and also knowing that they were first-generation, I was really amazed. I was like, "How did you do it?" And they're like, "Well, mainly by getting together with other undocumented students, helping each other and sharing books and strategies..."

Daniela also highlighted her friendships with other undocumented students as an important source of support and information about how to apply for scholarships and find other sources of financial support. She was motivated to continue because she knew actual undocumented that had earned a B.A. and were pursuing graduate studies:

I know people who have graduated from college, and...the experiences of all of us have been very similar, as far as how to pay for school, as far as how to apply for certain programs....One person that I met, he actually graduated. He's about to start a Master's program, and he told me that...you know, just keep doing what I'm doing...he told me to keep applying for scholarships,...if I can, try to find people who would be willing to finance my education because that's also one of the ways to do things.

By connecting with undocumented peers through college clubs and community youth organizations, the students were able to reduce their sense of alienation and, in turn, develop supportive relationships. Irene, for example, learned that by participating in or establishing undocumented student support groups, many undocumented students can band together and share resources and encourage each other during difficult times.

Academic Outreach Programs

Due to their high grades, many students were invited to participate in academic enrichment programs. These programs were an important resource for undocumented students like Thalia, who joined PUENTE, a program that provided access to caring counselors and professors. Linda also enjoyed the extensive support of the PUENTE program on her campus:

> My first year I met an English instructor that introduced me to the PUENTE Program, which helps minority students who want to go to a four-year college, who want to transfer. We visited universities like UC Santa Barbara, Berkeley, and private schools. They also gave me a $1000 scholarship, which paid for my tuition. My PUENTE counselor has been helping me with letters of recommendation for scholarships.

Lisa and Jairo also credit the PUENTE program for their academic success at the community college. Through the program they received advice about how to select transfer colleges and develop better study habits as Jairo explained:

> I got into the PUENTE program and that has helped me tremendously. They're always on top of you, in a good way because they want you to do good. And they will stay after class and talk to you. And we will have discussions and take trips to other universities. And we always talk about social issues dealing with Latinos and Hispanics. They really keep you on top of your game.

Like many students, Paulina' decision to attend a community college was driven by economic necessity. When she began to take courses, she did not feel intellectually challenged. When she serendipitously learned about the Honors program, Paulina decided to apply:

> I felt like community college was high school part two. I wasn't being challenged, and then a friend of mine whom I had met in one of my classes told me about the honor's track. I said, what's so good about it? And he's like, it's just like a lot of more rigorous work. It's not just one piece of paper and then you're done. And I was like, really? So I went and checked it out, and it was work, work, work. So I applied for it.

Although many academic programs on college campuses require proof legal residence, undocumented students were able to participate in those that did not require verification of their immigration status. Students found these programs to be instrumental in fostering their sense of mattering and empowerment. In all, 13 participants, such as Irene, described the support they received from programs such as AVID, Puente, SHPE, MESA, and other similar programs, "There are some programs that will help you…there are people who are willing to help you if you're willing to go on. So I think that's something that's really good about this campus." The accessibility of student services programs was a sign of validation (Rendón, 1994) for students like Valerie, who stated, "Right now I am part of the MESA (Mathematics, Engineering, & Science Achievement) program…MESA also gives lots of opportunities, like touring universities and things like that. They also give you information on scholarships and how to apply." Academic support programs fostered student academic development and provided some financial resources. Participants were able to expand their social support networks and learn more about the few available resources by participating in these programs.

Campus Life

Although much of the literature on community colleges cites the lack of supportive resources, some students like Thalia, reported positive views of their campus, "Everybody thinks it's a bad college because it's in the ghetto but I am there and I am succeeding. I think it's a good college with some really good professors." Isabel also reported a similar positive experience at her community college even though she had to travel a long distance to get to campus:

> Distance-wise it's pretty far and I could easily just stay at my local community college, but I really like the environment here. I had teachers that really worked with you to get things done and if you have trouble they'll help you out.

Jacqueline liked the guidance she received at her community college, "They offered lots of good things for undocumented students. They guided me very well. It really made me feel like I had an opportunity in my life and I wasn't just stuck there." Karen enjoyed meeting new people and interacting with her professors:

> It's been absolutely wonderful. I think I've learned a lot more things. It's a great experience. I never thought it'd be this great. I've met new people. I have more communications with teachers than I thought I would have and it's a great environment too.

Paulina had nothing but superlatives to describe her community college. She liked the diversity and the support and encouragement she received:

> The English department is the best. It's also very racially diverse. I only have good things to say about it. Although it might not be seen as one of the best junior colleges anywhere, I think it is. I have learned so much. And the people there are interested in me getting out of there and doing something with my life. Not just being there forever and ever.

Achievement Motivation

A prevalent theme in the interviews with the community college students was their sense of drive and determination. Even though for many the community college route was not their first choice, they were intent on succeeding. For example, Beatriz was motivated to prove people wrong about undocumented students, "I probably have more motivation because of my status. It makes it so much harder that I think I have to prove people wrong. And is not only that, I also want to do it for myself." Carla concurred when we asked if her status made her reconsider her college plans, "No, not at all. It's actually encouraging. It's such a challenge that I want to complete it." Carla sees a college degree as an accomplishment that transcends her legal marginality:

> I want to be educated because that's something that no one can take away from me. I'm the first one in my family to come here and to actually pursue something, like have a dream for this and work. I want to make my family very, very proud.

A second source of motivation for community college undocumented students was seeing and hearing about the hardships encountered by their parents in their physically-demanding jobs. Students aspire to get better jobs through education so they can help and take care of their parents. Daniela was inspired by her parents' work ethic and perseverance:

> What motivates me is seeing my parents work. My parents work really, really hard. I've seen my parents work so hard in sweat shops, restaurants. Just seeing my parents work so hard and coming home complaining about how hard they had worked, their pain and their suffering, that keeps me going. I feel like, "Wow, I'm not doing that." What they have to do every day, wake up early in the morning and come back home at night is way worse. I just feel that I have been given a little bit more than they have, so that to me just makes me think, "Well, I just got to work with what I got to make my parents' situation a little bit better."

Karen wants her parents to be proud of her, "I want to feel good about myself. I want people, my family especially, to feel good about me, to know that I was doing it, that I wanted to it." Esperanza was similarly motivated by her mother's and sister's hardships, a fate she hoped to avoid by getting a college education:

> I saw what my mom was going through with my father and saw my sister at a young age getting married, already having a kid, and I'm like, "I don't want this for me. I want something better because I know that if they brought me here for something better, I'm going to have to find it myself..." there is one thing that mom always tells me, "Struggle right now and later you will get something back."

Isabel did not want her parents sacrifice to bring her to the U.S. to be in vain:

> They came here and they struggled with three children...Not everybody has the guts to go through that and bring your

family with you in those circumstances...they brought us so we could educate ourselves and have a better opportunity...that's why I'm doing what I'm doing because I don't want their effort to be in vain.

Community college students also demonstrated perseverance in their attitudes about coursework. Isabel was very strategic in how she approached her school work, "So I guess in order to really get through it you have to want it badly, to say, 'OK, you know what? I'm passing this class. I'm going to do my best and stay committed to it.'" One of the most compelling stories of determination and perseverance was shared by Esperanza:

> It doesn't matter if I have to repeat my class, it doesn't matter if I have to work more hours at work to pay the money, to pay again for that math class. I also know that if I put more effort and work for it, I am going to pass it and I am going to be able to go to a higher level...I don't see myself dropping school. Even if it takes me longer to finish my career, but as long as I keep on going to school, I'm happy and I know that I'll be making my mom happy too.

Positive Reframing

Another psychosocial mechanism that helped participants was positive reframing (Suarez-Orozco & Suarez-Orozco, 1995). They found ways to focus their motivation by comparing their possible futures with peers that had made poor life choices, or by comparing their options and possibilities with those they saw as less fortunate, or those who faced more obstacles and challenges, or by drawing inspiration from those in similar circumstances that persevered. For example, Isabel's positive reframing helped her minimize the effect of various stressors in her life:

> I'll see, like on the side of the freeway, there's a Latino, or there's someone there trying to sell flowers or fruit instead of just asking for money...they're the ones that inspire me, because even they came here leaving their families behind,

leaving their culture behind for a better future...They're like my inspiration.

Students' ability to reframe their educational experiences positively and interpret their limited educational options in an optimistic manner seemed to be an effective coping mechanism for them (Gallimore & Reese, 1999; Suarez-Orozco & Suarez-Orozco, 1995). In spite of negative stereotypes, living in poor communities often inspired them to continue their education. Students described feeling fortunate to have opportunities to get ahead and vowed not to make poor decisions in their life, like many of their peers or classmates, that might cause them to miss those rare options available to them. Participants regularly reminded themselves of the "mistakes" of their peers. Like Irene, many shared how the bad choices made by their peers proved to be a "scared straight" strategy for them, "Some of my friends, my girlfriends, are pregnant, and they're in gangs, or some are dead, so it's like...I think I'm very fortunate." Carla added:

> My friends...they got involved with guys too early, so I used to see that. They started falling behind in their classes, and I was just so scared that I was like, "No way, that's not happening to me." So I tried even harder to stay committed to school.

Dulce was also motivated to do well in school and not become a teenage mother, "There are some girls I went to school with during high school...one in particular, she was my neighbor, and she already has two kids, and I don't know why she didn't pursue college." Isabel was determined not to join gangs:

> I would see how friends were into gangs or gang-related kinds of things. Some of them, yeah, they went to high school, but they didn't go far beyond high school...then some of the girls, the ones that were popular, they were all cute and the ones with the most boyfriends and stuff. They were the ones that would drop out faster, or end up getting married or having kids...the ones that were quieter and more into school are the ones that actually made it.

Carla, Dulce, Irene, and Isabel were all motivated to do well academically and avoid various peer pressures from observing the negatives choices made by some of their peers. Most described how they turned these negative peer experiences into life lessons. They described the negative consequences their peers were now facing due to bad life decisions and expressed determination not to make their lives more complicated by getting pregnant, joining gangs, or not pursuing a post-secondary education.

Gender Differences in Coping

Females students were more likely to disclose their status to others and seek support from peers and educators compared to their male counterparts. Male students were more likely to keep their status a secret because they did not want pity or be seen as vulnerable. Females, on the other hand, largely felt that sharing their secret was the only way to get the additional help they needed. In many cases, efforts resulted in additional forms of support and access to educational agents. Michelle felt like she had no other choice but to share her secret with others:

> I was sick of having to live underground all the time. It was just like, I'm going to start telling everybody about this. People were so uninformed. And I just decided to tell my professors; it came up with my counselors.

Liliana also felt that sharing her secret with others was the only way to get ahead, as she stated, "I just feel that if I put everything out there... I can say I feel this way because of my status, I feel the need to put everything out there in order to become someone." On the other hand, the male participants expressed a meritocracy ideal and a desire to do things on their own, and not receive "special" treatment that might diminish recognition of their own hard work. For example, Jason did not feel comfortable sharing his immigration status with anyone because he did not want to receive special treatment or pity. He did not want others to think that he was less capable:

> I don't want anybody to feel like I've achieved more just because of my status...That's one of the reasons I've kept it a

secret...I don't want to be flaunting my status: "Oh, I'm an immigrant and I'm better than you, and blah, blah, blah." I just want to be competitive and make sure I achieve a lot and prove to my parents that...I'm living the American dream, going to college, and I'm going to become somebody.

Overall, both males and females expressed similar attitudes about their academic, financial, and legal status issues. However, females did exhibit a stronger sense of tenacity or what they described as "stubbornness." For example, when participants were asked to describe personal characteristics that were helpful in their academic endeavors Jimena replied, "I guess I am stubborn. When people put me down, like my counselor or my mom saying that I am not going to college, I don't listen to them." Miriam, added, "I'm very stubborn. I am very hard-working." Sexism was a salient theme for females. As a result, many felt an added pressure to constantly prove themselves to parents, teachers, counselors, and others.

Academic Ability Comparisons

To examine possible distinctions in how community college Latino students have coped with their difficult academic and socioemotional experiences, participants were grouped into three different academic performance groups; a high (3.6 or above), above average (3.0–3.5), or average GPA (2.9 or less) groups. As Table 4.2 indicates, the High GPA students were more likely to have less household responsibilities, and worked less hours in jobs during both high school and college than the above average an average GPA students. Whereas 80% of average GPA students worked 20 hours per week or more during college, only 50% of the students in the high GPA group did so. Statistically, differences in household responsibilities and hours worked during high school or college were not significant across all groups.

Although the survey data only suggest possible differences in the relationship between achievement and work demands, the interview data provide a similar and more concrete evidence for the negative correlation between hours worked per week and achievement. For instance, Rosa, who had a 2.0 GPA, had multiple obligations as a single mother and the sole income earner. The various demands on her time affected her academic performance as she noted:

> It's been hard. If it were up to me, I would just go to college to finish my career. I hate that I have to work. I hate that I'm unable to concentrate and put one hundred percent of my effort into school, because I know that if I did, I would have been done a long time ago...I don't come from a very wealthy family. I have no income or support from my family, so I have to work. I can't just go to school and finish my career. I have to come home and go to school at night. And I have a daughter too, so that's even more pressure.

Like Rosa, many of the participants in the average GPA group reported having to work long hours while in high school and college to help support themselves and their families. In another example, Liliana maintained a 2.8 GPA but felt she could have invested more time in her academic and social development if she did not have to work so many hours. She stated, "It's been hard because I really can't focus too much on my homework, and again, I really can't do any other activities after classes because I'm always working." Carla, a 2.7 GPA student, expressed her frustration about how some Americans were clueless about how much undocumented students struggle to juggle work and school, "I don't really think they recognize that we have to work long hours to be able to save up that money and then attend class early in the morning." Similar sentiments emerged in both the above average and high GPA groups, but they were not as salient as their average GPA group counterparts. In some cases, some of the participants took time off after graduating high school to work longs hours in order to save money for their college tuition. This practice was more typical for those in the above average and high GPA groups. Jacinto, a 3.3 GPA student, was one of those who took time off, "After high school, I took a year off. It was basically just work. I worked a lot. I was also just trying to get myself together. I worked full-time. The following year I started school and still worked full-time."

Those who were in the high GPA group were more likely to receive more financial support from their parents and receive more scholarships. For example, Michelle, a 3.7 GPA student, explained how she was able to pay for her tuition:

> Before I got here [college], I had to work for three years in order to save like $15,000 and I had about $4,000 in scholarships when I got here, and I got into McNair's program so that's been paying for school. And while I have been at this college, I have received more scholarships, and I have worked along the way. I did ask my mom for $3,000.

In another example, Monica, a 3.7 GPA student, was able to pay her way through community college with scholarships, "My counselor saw the potential in me...and so she helped me apply for a scholarship, and I got several smaller scholarships...that's how I was able to go to college without having to work." There were statistically significant differences in the levels of extracurricular participation between average GPA students and high GPA students. Whereas all the High GPA students had participated in at least one extracurricular activity, only 82% of the average GPA students had done so. On average the high GPA group had participated in 6 different extracurricular activities during the schooling years, compared to 3.7 for the average GPA students. The above average GPA student group did report significantly higher levels of perceived discrimination (M=3.5), and sense of societal rejection (M=5.21) compared to the average GPA group (M=2.45 & M=3.17 respectively). Groups did not differ in their educational aspirations. On average all three groups aspired to earn at least a Masters degree. Average GPA students, however, had significantly lower educational expectations (M=4.00) than the high GPA group (M=5.25). Whereas 75% of the high GPA students still expected to earn at least a Masters degree, only 22% of the average GPA did so. All three student groups reported similar high valuing of schooling but the average GPA group reported statistically significant lower levels of parental valuing of school (M=2.57) compared to the High GPA group (M=3.57). Whereas 100% of the high GPA group reported that their parents felt that education was either "important," or "very important," only 49% of the average GPA group reported the same.

Overall, student comparisons based on their academic achievement profiles reveals a negative relationship between academic achievement and hours worked per week, and a positive relationship with extracurricular participation, educational expectations, and parental valuing of schooling. When participants were asked to share their views on how they persevere in school while facing all the obstacles related to their legal status, Valerie, who had a 4.0 GPA, responded:

> I'm determined to do what I want. I have my goals set, and I just know that I need do whatever I can to obtain them. I think that I persevere; I just won't give up. Even if I have the biggest obstacle in front of me, I'll just try to jump right over it.

Dulce, who had a 3.8 GPA, added, "I have high expectations of myself, and maybe my parents did, too. I'm sure they do, and even if they don't, I wouldn't want to let them down." Guillermo, a student with an overall 3.7 GPA highlighted his determination as the key:

> My determination...even though at times I felt like... it was easy to give up, but I knew that I was worth more than that, that there was so much I was able to give, if only somebody would give me the opportunity to demonstrate it. I think my passion...having learned of my parents' struggle and the struggle of what it is to be an undocumented immigrant here, and an undocumented student.

Isabel, who had a 3.3 GPA, was also determined not to give up because she could not envision a future without a college education:

> I guess, some determination from my part, because I could have easily given up in the past. There will be times when I'm like, "Oh, you know what? I'm not going to go to school." But then I'll think about it—"What am I going to do if I don't go to school? I'm going to work for minimum wage?"—when I know I could do better. I'm capable of doing more than just

Table 4.2 Academic ability group comparisons

	High GPA (N=8) %	M	Above Average GPA (N=18) %	M	Average GPA (N=11) %	M	Total (N=37) %	M
Non-academic commitments								
Household responsibilities[c]	13	2.33	12	2.93	9	2.95		2.79
Hrs. work/wk in HS[d]	28	5.71	78	17.27	45	16.11	57	14.32
Hrs. work/wk in College[d]	50	16.29	73	35.42	80	30.38	70	28.96
Involvement								
Extracurricular Participation	100	6.00[a]	100	5.11[ab]	82	3.27[b]	95	4.77
Psychosocial								
Distress[e]	0	1.93	6	1.97	0	2.06	0	1.98
Discrimination[f]	0	2.98[ab]	0	3.50[b]	0	2.45[a]	0	3.12
Rejection due to Status[g]	25	4.19[ab]	65	5.21[a]	13	3.17[b]	31	4.49
School Attitudes								
Educational Aspirations[h]	100	5.57	83	5.53	66	5.00	76	5.41
Educational Expectations[h]	75	5.25[a]	66	4.78[ab]	22	4.00[b]	49	4.76
Valuing of Schooling[i]	75	6.60	84	6.14	72	5.85	79	6.18
Parental valuing of schooling[j]	100	3.57[a]	82	3.32[ab]	49	2.57[b]	85	3.20

*Column means that do not share a superscript are statistically different at the .05 level

[c] Scale range: 1-5. Percent reflects responses 4-5 combined.

[d] Hours worked per week in High School (HS) and College. Percent represents the proportion of those working more than 20 hours per week.

[e] Scale range: 1-4. Percent reflects responses 3-4 combined.

[f] Scale range: from 1 - 6. Percent reflects responses 5-6 combined.

[g] Scale range: from 1 - 7. Percent reflects responses 5-7 combined.

[h] Scale range: 1 *(graduate from high school)* - 6 *(J.D./Ph.D./M.D. degree)*. Percent reflects responses 5-6 combined.

[i] Scale range: 1 - 7. Percent reflects responses 6-7 combined.

[j] Scale range: 1-4. Percent reflects responses 3-4 combined.

that, so I keep myself back in. It might take me longer, it has, but I'm still here."

Carla, a 2.7 GPA student, was motivated to excel so she would be a competitive applicant for the few scholarships available for undocumented students. She stated, "It's scholarships...I feel like I have to do the best that I can, like I have to push myself to do the best, just because for money and scholarships, that's one way of getting them." Diego, a 2.4 GPA student, sees himself as a fighter. He remarked, "Going every single day and fighting for what I want to do. Even though I may have to go through these anti-immigrant legislations, I still 'gotta' wake up the next morning and try to survive and be a fighter." Rosa, a 2.0 GPA student, credits her positive attitude. She noted, "Having a positive attitude, not letting obstacles make you give up. I've had a lot of obstacles...One needs to learn how to overcome them. Take it day by day." In spite of the differences in grade point averages, the majority of the participants shared similar positive psychosocial characteristics and internal dispositions.

Community college undocumented Latino students work long hours to earn money to pay for school and help their families. Working many hours outside of school does seem to impact their academic performance somewhat and may also affect their educational goals, possibly as a result of increased hardship they experience managing work and school. One of the highlights for students at the community college is the level of support they receive from caring faculty, who often went above and beyond their formal roles as professors. Several students described these professors as "mentors." Students also benefited from the support they received from academic outreach programs. These programs became important sources of information on not only how to navigate the institutional bureaucracy, but also helped students develop concrete plans to transfer to the university. Through these programs, students also met other students who shared not only their educational goals but also some of the same hardships. The programs were often one of the few sources of scholarship money to pay for college. Finally, academic outreach programs provided students with more rigorous academic courses. Despite their initial disappointment at not being able to enroll directly in four-year universities, once they began attending, students reframed their experience in a positive way by highlighting the opportunities to meet new and diverse friends, positive experiences with professors, and access to resources specifically for undocumented students. They also emphasized the affordability of the community college.

Although they faced many obstacles and barriers as described in Chapter 3, students demonstrated great resilience and often coped with their obstacles by seeking support from parents, teachers, peers, and community agents. Compared to their male counterparts, female students were more likely to disclose their legal status to teachers and counselors to recruit their support. Male students were often uncomfortable sharing their immigration status. Despite an uncertain future, the most striking theme from the interviews was the tenacious optimism of students. Rather than become dejected, some students derived their motivation to continue with their studies from being undocumented. They reframed it as a challenge they were intent on overcoming. Even at the prospect of earning a college degree and not being able to use it, community college students underscored the sense of accomplishment from just becoming "educated," regardless of their possibilities for employment. Their valuing of a college degree as seminal milestone was reinforced by their working class parents who modeled a strong work ethic despite the hardship they endure in their physically demanding low-wage jobs. Students aspired to earn a college degree, even if they don't get to use it, because they wanted to make their parents proud. They saw their accomplishment as a way to repay their parents for all the sacrifices they had made to bring them to the United States to provide a better life and educational opportunities.

CHAPTER 5

Institutional Perspective on Students' Socioemotional Experiences

As undocumented students become more represented on college campuses, there is a growing concern among higher education practitioners about proper institutional practices. An increasing body of research suggests that in order for undocumented students to access and persist in higher education, educational practitioners and policymakers must possess an understanding of their unique experiences (Chavez et al., 2007; Oliverez, 2006). Undocumented students are far less likely to know the requirements necessary or the process of applying to college due to their lack of familiarity with the U.S. education system (Contreras et. al., 2008). To this end, research and practical resources have emerged to begin to address these issues (Miksch, 2005; University of California, Davis, 2008). It remains to be seen how these research efforts will translate (or not) into greater inroads on issues such as the availability of public financial aid for undocumented students—a challenge that nearly all recent studies of undocumented students' experiences in higher education have discussed as a key barrier to their transition to and persistence in college (Chavez et al, 2007). Undocumented students who are savvy enough to navigate high school and complete the requirements for college are still left with the considerable challenge of financing their college education.

Staff members are responsible for conveying the most up-to-date and accurate information to their students. Advisers, college counselors, financial aid staff, and outreach personnel are all on the front line of interacting with college students and a critical element of their position is to assist students with navigating college. Undocumented Latino students are the most vulnerable within the Latino college population and often are in most need of these services (Gandara & Contreras, 2009). From admissions and residency to making tuition payments, students find little coordination across administrative units and find themselves having to make multiple trips to offices in order to get their questions answered and their problems resolved. As increasing numbers of undocumented students make it to college, many develop interests in specialized programs in which they cannot earn the credential or final certification because they entail state exams that required U.S. government-issued IDs and background checks. Many campuses, however, do not offer students information on which programs have such requirements that may preclude them. Some students stumble across information on the Internet, often risking being misinformed. While some students have find their way through these administrative barriers, other are denied entry.

Community College Personnel

To contribute to the small but growing body of research on institutional capacity building to serve undocumented students, as well as to provide an institutional perspective on the challenges described by community college undocumented Latino students in this study, we interviewed eight community college professionals at five different institutions. We wanted to better understand how community colleges are providing services to undocumented students and whether efforts to increase access and retention had been developed in response to the challenges students face due to their status. We also wanted to understand institutional constraints in implementing services and programs to specifically help and support undocumented students. These guiding questions guided our qualitative analysis.

As Table 5.1 indicates, community college personnel sample included individuals who work in various capacities ranging from administration such as Dean of Students, to Counseling, frontline staff,

Institutional Perspective on Students' Socioemotional Experiences

and academic outreach professionals. Years of experience in their current position ranged from 3 years to 15 years. Although some described themselves as undocumented student advocates, others did not. Overall, community college staff confirmed much of the socioemotional distress and institutional challenges students described. They described negative and prejudiced attitudes from staff, financial concerns, lack of staff training and preparation, and lack of centralized information and services. The few resources available included, some institutional aid, a small but growing network of advocates, and student support groups. Following is a detailed discussion of the main findings.

Table 5.1 Community College Personnel Interview Participants

Pseudonym	Current position	Years in position	College Pseudonym
Rick	Academic Affairs	15 years	Emerald CC
Dennis	School Relations Coordinator	5 years	Orange CC
Rita	Dean of Admissions	6 years	Orange CC
Gail	Clerical	12 years	Metro CC
Jessica	Honors Program Counselor	6 years	Coast CC
Adriana	Dean of Students	3 years	Orange CC
Linda	Director of Student Affairs	7 years	Mountain CC
John	Academic Counselor	15 years	Emerald CC

Social, emotional, and psychological concerns

Sixty-three percent of community college staff described fear, shame, guilt, feelings of not belonging, loneliness and, hopeless as the main concerns for undocumented community college students. Like many of the student interviews, Adriana, the Dean of Students at Orange CC also described the despair experienced by many undocumented student's that did not learn about their status until they began applying for college:

I know of their struggles. It breaks my heart to see that we have students who oftentimes don't realize that they're undocumented until it's time to pursue higher education. I know so many of those cases where they want to apply for a scholarship or they want to apply for technician and then that's when their parents are honest with them and tell them what the reality is. So they're heartbroken.

Rick, an academic affairs professional at Emerald CC described the sense of shame and guilt students feel:

There's also a lot of shame and guilt and feeling isolated in that they think that they are the only one, even now with all that we do to promote the services for our undocumented students. There's a lot of either shame or guilt in using those services because…how other people view them is how they've internalized viewing themselves, that they shouldn't even be getting any services because they're undocumented and have no right to these kinds of services.

Linda, a Director of Student Affairs at Mountain CC described the sense of hopelessness and loneliness students often expressed to caring staff:

In most cases, I feel like they feel alone and they feel like there's no one that can help them, even though I say, "I'm here to be your advocate or I want to help you or I want to see you succeed," they still feel like, "That's great, but you can't help me because nobody can help me." So I would say loneliness is huge, lack of support, and then hopelessness.

Adriana, the Dean of Students at Orange CC sensed anger and frustration from students, she noted, "In some students I've seen anger…the sense of unfairness, 'It's not fair that I didn't ask to come here, I was brought here by my parents.'" John, an Academic Counselor at Emerald CC thinks that fear is a constant concern for students:

They are fearful that they can't trust anyone or that anyone can understand them. I'm sure that it can go as deep as students being depressed...they're also dealing with the law too and this constant fear...Am I going to be deported? Do I have to worry about my family being deported?" That is a constant fear...they don't feel permanent...any day it's possible that things can change.

Negative Staff Attitudes

The initial contact with the community college is often complicated by various socioemotional concerns. Among these is the pervasive negative attitudes about undocumented students throughout the community college. John described negative and prejudiced staff attitudes as a major obstacle for undocumented students:

> They're dealing with racism, just dealing with the ins and outs of micro aggressions on a daily basis of hearing their professors talking about supporting the bill in Arizona or, "being against illegal immigration." You know, it might not necessarily be specifically directed at them...the teacher's not necessarily sitting in front of them saying, 'You,' but making...general statements ...on a daily basis where they have to deal with racism in their face.

In addition to one-sided classroom discussions on immigration that frame immigrants as lawbreakers or undesirable, 63% of interviewees also described general attitudes among student services personnel that students should not be allowed to enroll. Rita, the Dean of Admissions at Orange CC stated, "There are some people out there who just believe they shouldn't be here and are not happy about it." Adriana described staff negative attitude as the main hurdle in providing services to students, "Well, I think that the main issue...is working with individuals that do not understand or are not sensitive...I have tried to bring that up and it has been a very controversial issue." John has also heard similar sentiments on his campus, "I've definitely heard, 'Well, they're not citizens so why are we bending over backwards to help this group that aren't citizens?'" Most of the participants described resistance to providing services to undocumented students as "under the radar" and always publicly articulated. For example, when Linda described some of the staff attitudes at her campus she noted:

> The resistance is a little bit quiet because I think people feel uncomfortable saying that they're resistant to it, but there's certainly the feeling that we have students who are here legally, who are documented, who are experiencing the same kinds of troubles, so why are we going out of our way for people who are in essence breaking the law and here illegally? So that's one sentiment and it's very kind of under the carpet. People don't verbalize it, but you can tell who those people are.

Students encounter additional challenge when staff let their prejudice inform their practices despite state law. Adriana believes that on her campus, undocumented students are turned away by prejudiced personnel that refuse to allow undocumented students to apply for admissions under AB540, the California in-state tuition law:

> the admissions office ... they don't want to interpret AB540 for what it's intended to be and have set up their own interpretation of it and their own requirements...they have a sense of what it's supposed to be, but they don't follow the law.

Adriana expressed concern about these practices because she thinks it makes students feel rejected, "My biggest concern is...how they must feel mistreated...my perception is that they probably don't feel very welcomed by the first office that they come into, the admissions office." The interviews with CC personnel suggested that undocumented students have various reasons for feeling fearful, ashamed, lonely, and that they do not belong on campus. The environment can range from not being entirely welcoming to being quite hostile.

Enrollment

The socioemotional concerns of undocumented students are driven by their negative encounters with prejudiced personnel, beginning with their initial efforts to enroll. Their fear of being "found out" can become more intense at the community college which can discourage them from seeking enrollment. Dennis also shared Adriana's sentiment that student's feelings about not feeling welcomed, in addition to their parents' fears, discourages them from enrolling:

> They are a little apprehensive about going to complete the application and they also do not feel that they'd be welcomed in approaching... A lot of students feel that they do not belong just because...of their status...also they're a little apprehensive and afraid to disclose their status to others...Some of the parents are afraid that if their students go to school, somehow they will find out that they do not have documents.

For those brave enough to venture into the admissions office, the application process can be daunting and overwhelming as Jessica described:

> They're scared and confused about the processing... there's a lot of things they don't know, that they have to fill out additional paperwork, the Nonresident Tuition Exemption form and once they do get it in their hands, they don't know what to mark because the technical language is a bit confusing.

Adriana and Jessica felt that having to provide so much documentation discourages students and becomes an enrollment barrier. Other times, students may also get misinformation during the enrollment process as Rick explained:

> I've heard a lot of students say that they were given incorrect information, were not given complete information about what to do to have the AB540 status, so they end up applying as an

out-of-state student, which means they have to pay $200 whatever for the fees and then they realize, "Oh, I'm that status. This is what I need to do," after they've talked to someone other than admissions.

Unfortunately, many students don't get to that point. They don't even know that college is an option or that they are eligible for in-state tuition rates.

Institutional Challenges

According to Adriana, the barriers to higher education access for undocumented students at most community colleges are driven by three factors, "I think partially it's the lack of support, partially it's the lack of knowledge, and partially it's our AB540 students still not feeling comfortable within the environment." There was consensus that the biggest barrier for community college undocumented students is a lack of financial resources. All personnel interviewed indicated financial concerns as an ongoing stressor for students. Oftentimes students don't even realize they're not eligible for financial aid until they arrive on campus to enroll. Jessica felt that the lack of financial aid can negatively impact student motivation:

> being able to pay for college is the largest obstacle I've seen...they know they can't get financial aid and be eligible for it, but they don't know where they're going to get the money, so it pretty much kills their motivation or can kill their motivation.

Economic challenges also impact academic progress for students. They often have to drop courses in order to keep jobs that will allow them to continue to pay for their schooling, as was the case for a student that Gail had met with the day before the interview, "she was on progress probation because she dropped some courses again. She works, she had to...drop the courses to keep the job." According to Gail, the contrast between the experiences of low-income students who are eligible for financial aid, and their undocumented counterparts is very clear:

the difference between a regular student who comes from a similar...low socioeconomic background as students who are AB540 is...they get financial aid, work study, they work on campus, at the same time go to school, so this allows students more flexible schedules so they can do better academically, versus students who are AB540 who don't qualify for work study, they have to work late night shift, graveyard shift, heavier job, and at the same time trying to keep their grades up, which is mostly hard. I've seen students falling asleep during the class because they had to work all night and then come to school in the mornings.

Adriana expressed frustration in not having any institutional options to help undocumented students financially in the same way that she is able to help other low-income students:

> Just breaks my heart...I have three students in mind right now that ...I struggle with...how can I help the students financially? They're working and they're doing a great job...I don't know of a way that I could compensate them the way I'm able to compensate other students.

In addition to affecting their performance in the classroom, undocumented students are also limited in their ability to become involved in campus activities. Adriana described a scenario that has become increasingly prevalent in the emerging literature on undocumented students in higher education:

> There's the financial issue, which is I think the biggest hurdle... I'm sure that you in your research are very familiar with the students who will work for a semester, then will raise enough money for that following semester to pay for their books, and then they have to take off the next semester...and it's a cycle and it takes them a lot longer. I have students, brilliant students, who want to be in student government or who want to be in our Ambassador Program and I can't pay them because they're AB540.

John also expressed a similar observation on his campus:

> they may want to be a full-time student, but they can't because they might have to work and they work under the table just to help out with family, but they want to be a full-time student and take part in school and all the activities, but really can't because they maybe have to go to work or go home and help their brother or sister.

As Adriana's and John's examples highlight, not only do students struggle saving enough money to pay for tuition and books, but they also miss out on important student development activities that are an important part of the college-going experience, such as extracurricular participation. In addition to financial hardship, fear of being "found out" also plays a role in students' hesitation to get involved on campus as Rick explained, "I think fear is probably the most common element, and even now we have students that will not participate in activities because they think they might be 'found out.'"

Undocumented students face many of the same challenges that students who are the first in their family to enroll in college encounter: they often come from low-income families, have graduated from high schools that did not prepare them well academically and they have to navigate an unfamiliar and complicated bureaucracy of higher education. John explained some of the challenges typical of first generation students:

> One of the difficulties is just knowing what college is about and how to navigate through the system—what is an AA degree, what is an AS degree, how do I transfer, how do I come up with a major?...with first-generation students it's just a little bit more challenging because they don't have necessarily parents or brothers or sisters that they can ask those kind of questions at home. So right at the beginning I think is where the process starts to get a little bit challenging for students.

Although many schools have programs in place to support working-class and first generation students through this difficult transition, undocumented students are often not eligible for these services and programs, as Gail, a clerical staff at Metro CC explained, "Students who are undocumented ...are not eligible for services through EOPS, so mostly we see a lot of the students applying for help, hoping to get some kind of support from resources available, but unfortunately, they don't qualify." Another significant challenge for undocumented students at the community college is the lack of identifiable resources and support systems on campus, even when they do exist. Jessica explained:

> They don't know where to go if they have a question a lot of times about how to fill out a form. They don't know who to go to within the community college...when they have questions about how to do something properly...because it's a very private matter.

Rick, noted a similar scenario on his campus:

> I think even though we offer different kinds of services to AB540 students, it's still almost like a secret club. Not a secret, but like an underground club. It would be really nice to just let the campus know, "Here's an office where AB540 students can go." Like it's in the schedule of classes, it's on our website, all those things.

Despite an increase in scholarships that do not preclude undocumented students, information about applying can be elusive and complicated that even academically talented students struggle with all the required steps to apply. Despite their availability students are not aware that they do not require a social security number.

Lack of training

A major obstacle undocumented students face in accessing higher education is that school- and college-based professionals are not trained to provide guidance, information, and support to them. There is a need for systematic education of K-12 and higher education professionals about the postsecondary opportunities available to undocumented students (Oliverez, 2007). In our sample, there was a consensus that community college staff are not properly trained to be responsive to the specific needs of undocumented students. Although many community college personnel are sympathetic and work diligently to help students, they often are not able to help students. Linda for example, didn't know how to help a high achieving student who was having a difficult time after the realization that she would not be able to attend the university she was admitted to:

> One case…was accepted to her first-choice for a university and couldn't go there because there was no way she could afford it, so that was followed by hopelessness, "I can't do anything. I'm not going to be successful. This is never going to change," and to be honest with you, I'm not sure how to deal with that.

John noted that the counseling staff at his institution was also lacking in information and training and that most manage as best they can on their own:

> It's a counseling matter and I certainly would hope that we can discuss that in counseling meetings, but as mentioned, I don't think that there's enough information for those that lead the meetings to really come with a wealth of information…Right now, it kind of feels like, "Well, to each his own," and you kind of have to do research on your own to find this information out, which I think is sad because that's not what we're doing with everybody else.

Although some staff are well-informed, most are not. Rita had a knowledgeable staff member that ensured that undocumented students received the proper information. Gail on the other hand, didn't feel properly informed. When asked if she had received any training to work with undocumented students she responded, "No, I haven't and I wish I did." When asked how prepared she felt to work with undocumented students she answered, "Probably very little." Knowledgeable staff like Jessica often have to make individual efforts to become informed:

I definitely make sure to do my homework and find out as much information as possible, so I feel like I'm a good resource because I go out of my way to learn about how to help the students...I'll go out of my way to make sure I have the precise information.

Rick also had to learn how to help undocumented students on his own. Dennis does his own research, looks for publications on the Internet and tries to learn from others that are supportive of undocumented students. Out of all the staff we interviewed, only Adriana reported that she had received formal training to work with undocumented students. She and others on her campus attended a training event held at a different institution.

Gildersleeve (2010) argues that current college-going practices for undocumented students are often marked by serendipity rather than by institutionalized effort, noting that schools, colleges, and communities do not operate systematically to foster postsecondary access for this population. Undocumented students who are enrolled in colleges and universities are most likely there because of exceptional practices of educators who intervened in their K-12 schooling experiences (Gildersleeve, 2009, 2010; Gutierrez, Hunter, & Arzubiaga, 2009).

Advocates

Many of the faculty and staff who make individual efforts to learn about how to provide better services and support to undocumented students often become key allies and advocates. They play a critical role in supporting undocumented students in a variety of ways. Jessica helps her student strategize and plan ahead:

> I'll tell them, "Make a separate appointment with me so we can talk about how to apply for scholarships and how we're going to fund it..."if we have the time I tell them, "You know, you might want to think about maybe fundraising." I've even talked to students about car washes, about how they can start early to make money on their own to have money when they transfer.

She also draws on her social networks to help students find legal advice. When students have legal questions, she draws on her circle of immigration attorney friends to refer students. Self-described advocates reported that in order to become effective advocates, they first had to earn trust from the students as Linda explained:

> I think I do a good job of convincing them that it's OK to tell their story once I get a student to trust me. I think I do well to get the students to trust me, that I'm going to be an advocate and I'm not going to hurt them. And then after that, convincing them to allow me to tell their story to other people who might be able to help them.

Adriana also considers herself and advocate for undocumented students on her campus. When she learns that a particular student is having a difficult time with another administrator or a staff member, she steps in to try to help, even when it creates interpersonal tension between her and her coworkers. She described a small network of campus staff that work together to support students:

> There's a good network of us, of administrators and professionals here at this college that have learned to work together and as soon as we find out about our research, we tell each other about it...We have some counselors that I work with...a counselor in EOPS who is knowledgeable on the AB540 requirements and works with the students to get them in here and then helps them transfer.

Despite these efforts, Adriana lamented not being able to do more for students:

> I'm a good advocate for AB540 students, but I wish that I could be a stronger advocate...I wish that I had the time to be able to explore more things that are out there...services, programs, organizations that are willing to help AB540 students.

Student advocates often worry about protecting students from unsupportive or prejudiced staff. Rick explained:

> I think politically we're afraid to kind of be open about it because there's so much criticism, especially right now with the political situation about undocumented individuals that I think we're being protective of the students...I think if I do that, I'm kind of exposing them.

Advocates also worry about that students might disclose their status to the wrong person on campus so they advice students to consult them first before disclosing their status to other staff and they try to keep a list of trusted allies that can provide particular information or support. Even though students do not qualify for many of the campus services for low-income or first generation college students, at Jessica's campus, many of the staff from these programs work as advocates and allies for undocumented students:

Existing Resources and Support

The efforts of allies and advocates over the years have resulted in a small but growing menu of services and support for undocumented students. Oftentimes, advocates have to overcome a variety of institutional obstacles to implement services. One of the challenges of increasing financial support for students on campus is a concern about breaking the law. When a student organization at Linda's institution tried to set up a scholarship program, the financial aid office said it was illegal to specify that it was only for undocumented students. they had to reword the eligibility language to include other students. Another strategy that Linda described her institution employs is using the FAFSA with undocumented student but only for internal purposes to match undocumented students with unrestricted institutional aid.

Community colleges have also improved their efforts to disseminate information about scholarships and other types of financial assistance to undocumented students. Jessica noted:

> The Student Services side of my campus... tends to be conscious of the fact that we have undocumented students and

they tend to be somewhat proactive, like we'll get emails about different opportunities for AB540 students or scholarships that come from counseling or Student Services and we get some information that's sent out from the state.

Oftentimes, however, the scholarship amounts are modest and the amount and the number of scholarships are not enough according to Rick, "We do give scholarships, small ones, for tuition and books and vouchers...books, things like that, but it's not enough, it's never enough for the number of students."

In addition to financial aid, campuses have developed other resources for students, including access to academic support programs, student clubs, and various "unofficial" services. Academic outreach programs that do not exclude undocumented students, oftentimes become critical sources of information and guidance. Another important source of support for students on campus is student organizations. Adriana commended the student organization on campus for providing students with much needed peer support, "they have done an excellent job within the last four years. It's a large group and they take on the role of also putting on some events." Other campuses were taking steps to start undocumented student clubs.

Various campuses also employed a variety of creative and "unofficial" strategies to help students. At Linda's campus, caring and supportive staff also help students with basic necessities such as food and housing:

> I work in an office where the staff is very understanding of that situation so at one point I remember the secretary in the office bought a lot of frozen items that she kept in a freezer in her office, so whenever these students came, if they were hungry, we could actually offer them food...In Student Services, the Student Service managers...have gift cards to the different eateries on campus...we call it the emergency fund, so if there's a student who really has a need and doesn't have anything to eat, we can offer that type of support...in the Student Life office, we keep a list of local shelters where you can go spend the night if you don't have anywhere to stay and resources for students who are homeless. In some cases, there

have been AB540 students who couldn't pay the rent or they lost a job. So we do try to provide services, but they're not official. You wouldn't find them in a manual or a catalog.

Linda and her staff also help students find jobs:

> Also we...try and find jobs for them, jobs that they didn't have to have documentation, for example tutoring. One of the students I worked with who was a math major...we would find him tutoring jobs for math and people would pay him for one hour at a time or two hours at a time.

Despite a lack of training, some community colleges are developing and improving efforts to provide college-going information to undocumented students before they graduate from high school. Advocates and allies work to inform college recruiters before they visit high school campuses so they inform high school counselors and can answer specific questions from undocumented students about the in-state tuition law, and specific enrollment procedures. Staff noted that some high school counselors were well-informed about the issue and passed on information about in-state tuition to students while they were still in high school.

Needed Resources and Support

Although efforts to support undocumented students have increased, the interview data suggests much work remains to be done. Some of the more important needs mentioned included, more funding, undocumented-student-specific centralized services that are widely-publicized, and staffed by "trusted" individuals, more allies and advocates, properly trained and knowledgeable personnel, and increased outreach to students while they're still in high school. Gail asserted the need for additional institutional funding. Linda highlighted the need to increase services:

> It's really difficult for me to find services because in many instances, I've had different students come to me and they don't have money, they can't have a job, they can't pay their

tuition, some literally are hungry and somehow they need to eat, and there's not a whole lot we can do...I would really like to have more resources to be able to refer them to, more information in terms of what is out there.

Most agreed that students remained underserved needed to have more services tailored to undocumented students' needs that were widely publicized, and run by supportive staff. Jessica noted:

I don't feel like we're getting to all of them. I don't feel like they know who to go to. They sometimes get mixed information that's not always accurate...there's not an AB540 office at our campus, you know, so they have to know who's going to be friendly...there isn't a central place to get this information...at each campus there should be someone who students know that they can go to for their questions, like a central resource for AB540 students...that students know that they can go to and it's a trusted person.

There was some concern that a centralized-services office might make students feel too exposed or publicly visible and might make them apprehensive about visiting or using its services. Providing a "safe" space that students could easily learn about would require a delicate balance according to Linda:

The most helpful service I think would be a safe place where undocumented students can feel comfortable saying, "I need help," and not being afraid of being deported...where they don't have to be afraid to tell their story, that's what I come across over and over, is that they're afraid to tell their story.

The need for more undocumented student allies and advocates among community college staff was also highlighted. Allies were viewed as important sources of social and emotional support for students who are fearful of deportation or for those that feel that they have no one at the community college with their secret. Similarly both knowledgeable and supportive staff were noted as important institutional goals. Most staff are not familiar with important details about the in-state tuition law, don't know which programs and services undocumented students are eligible for and which ones they're not, and don't know how to help a distraught undocumented student that may be in need of psychosocial and emotional support. Informed staff was viewed as a powerful message to undocumented students: that they matter and that they are not viewed as being inferior to other students. Without formal training, Linda thought that formal training would make a significant difference in helping staff feel more comfortable to work with undocumented students:

> The people who are uncomfortable with it, it's only because they don't know what to do...I've seen where a student might come in crying and kind of tell their whole story to a staff member and the staff member feels bad for the student, but is uncomfortable because he or she just does not know what the next step should be or how to handle it. So I think that's where the training piece would come in. If we could train people on how to deal with undocumented students or AB540 students and kind of teach them, "This is the next step or this is what we can do," and really empower people with information, I think it would be great.

Finally, community college personnel expressed the need to increase efforts o provide information to students during high school. Dennis lamented, "AB540 students first need to be informed and I think the parents and the school administrators at the high school level need to be informed that there is an AB540 law. A lot of times they're not." Rick also noted that in order to reduce student fear, it was also important to involve and educate parents about their child's higher education options:

> I think it's important...to involve their parents. A lot of their fears come from what their parents have taught them in order to survive, "Don't talk about this. Don't tell anyone." It's kind of a secret sort of thing, which is just for survival of course, but if the parents also know that there is a support system, I think it helps them support their child in continuing their education.

Optimism and Uncertainty

Despite the various challenges the undocumented students face, some interviewees described the psychological resilience that has been noted in the research literature (Pérez et al., 2009). Jessica observed that although she had met undocumented students who were "quick to drop out," when faced with challenges, she also noted that many other students persevered:

> they actually are super resilient...they have an overall really positive attitude about it and they have to. I think that's the only reason why they survive. So I don't meet students that are really bummed out..it allows them to get through the system and still be motivated. So overall, they have really positive outlooks and they're very highly motivated, oftentimes more motivated.

Nevertheless, while they enjoy a small but growing number of resources and supportive staff in some campuses, John lamented that students still worry about their future as unemployable college graduates:

> You may have students that are dealing with issues of anger and frustration where it's, "Wow, we go and get a good education and I don't have to pay nonresidential fees, but then I can't get a job." You know, I think that would make anyone frustrated and angry... It's a challenge for students to be AB540 because, yes, you can come to school, but when it's time for you to get a job, it's difficult to get a job or they're nonexistent, and so students seem to be a little confused as to how can education really benefit them monetarily if they can't use their education to find a job.

Community Colleges and Higher Education Access

Overall, this chapter provides an institutional perspective on the challenges faced by Latino undocumented community college students. Interviewees felt they have not been properly trained by their institutions to work with undocumented students. Many interviewees who work closely with undocumented students, for example, could not explain what the California in-state tuition law, also known as AB540, is and the criteria and paperwork used to help students become eligible. Those who directly provide services to students made an effort to find information and resources on their own but their knowledge about the issue remains limited. Most interviewees said that they would like to: (a) get formal training which currently doesn't exist and (b) have a one-stop shop campus/online resource site they can consult for information and resources to better serve undocumented students. Interviewees, felt that if formal training to work with undocumented students is implemented, to be effective it should be institutionalized and made mandatory for all school personnel. Interviewees also confirmed that most campus support services that are available to low-income students are not available to undocumented students.

Although allies and advocates have helped to create support structures, community college personnel noted that these institutions needed to increase their efforts ensure that their mission of higher education access for historically marginalized groups include undocumented students. Adriana proclaimed:

> Our role is to educate and to provide access to students who are seeking education and when we put those obstacles in the way, we've become something else...I follow the law and I'm not saying we need to cut corners...but I also think that we don't have to assert undue obstacles.

Overall, we found that some community colleges have implemented various efforts to recruit, enroll, and support undocumented students while other have taken few efforts if any. In those campuses students are more fearful about disclosing their status or asking for support.

Implications for Institutional Practice

Since the community college system is the preferred "gateway" for many undocumented students due to its open door policy and affordability, these institutions must play an important role in educating and serving this population. Thus, community colleges need to pay close attention to the behavior, attitudes, and challenges of undocumented students (Dozier, 1995; Pérez, Cortés, Ramos, Coronado, 2010). Although school officials may not readily know who is undocumented, intervention strategies should be implemented to help students seek the academic and social support necessary without fear or threat. Effective college outreach and recruitment efforts need to consider the ways in which undocumented students are systematically excluded from participation in college-going activities due to their undocumented status, language, and unfamiliarity with the American educational system. All these forms of exclusion demonstrate that new methods of outreach and recruitment are required by colleges and universities that explicitly target undocumented students. By simply recognizing the needs of undocumented students, student affairs practitioners can begin to create outreach efforts that intentionally take their specific situations into account (Gildersleeve & Ranero, 2010). The following section provides a detailed discussion of some of the effective practices that can be used.

Training College Faculty and Staff

School personnel must be trained in how to respond to the diverse needs of the growing college-ready undocumented student population as these students deal with a unique set of challenges resulting from their residency status. Once teachers, counselors, admissions staff, financial officers, and registrars are better informed about options available to undocumented students, they will be well-equipped to educate, counsel, and support them at each point along the college pipeline (Oliverez, 2007). Specifically, institutional agents should be trained to be sensitive to the needs of this population. On many occasions, undocumented students have been scrutinized and humiliated simply because they did not furnish a social security number. Students develop great anxiety when they seek services at the front counter of an admissions and records office because student services personnel are not adequately trained to work with this population. A comprehensive training workshop on undocumented students can greatly improve services to these students.

Informed student support program counselors can become advocates and important sources of information for undocumented students (Brilliant, 2000). Counselor collaboration with instructional faculty and student support program leaders would be beneficial in order to provide helpful referrals to students. Motivated undocumented students need to know about honors programs, student-run organizations, and alternative sources of financial aid. This information can help reduce stress for undocumented students (Pérez, Cortés, Ramos, Coronado, 2010).

It is critical that campus faculty and staff be informed about the policies and regulations affecting undocumented students. Taking the initiative to be informed and staying up-to-date on campus, state, and federal policies is one way for student affairs professionals to be prepared when approached by an undocumented student with a question or concern. Colleges should develop campus-wide initiatives to educate faculty and staff so they are able to support this unique student population. They should also develop campus-specific resource guides to help students navigate their educational experience at that campus. Initiatives that are currently in place in various colleges, particularly in California, resulted from the efforts of active student leaders' calls for campus initiatives to address their concerns (Hernandez, Hernandez, Gadson et al., 2010).

The more informed student affairs professionals are about the legal and policy contexts of undocumented students' lives, the better they can serve these students. When undocumented students see that student affairs professionals know about and demonstrate an ethic of care regarding their unique realities, it increases the students' opportunity and likelihood to develop trust with student affairs professionals. Students' trust can translate into a more engaged use of student support services, and perhaps even assist student affairs professionals in learning how better to support these students' academic achievement and personal growth (Gildersleeve, Rumann, & Mondragon, 2010).

College Outreach and Recruitment

College outreach and recruitment is another important area that requires new solutions to the admissions and matriculation difficulties of undocumented students. Since community colleges will likely be the first stepping-stone for most undocumented students, it is important to disseminate information about the matriculation process for undocumented students, scholarship and student services programs, and transfer information to high school institutional agents and their students. High school counselors can also encourage high-achieving undocumented students to take advantage of dual enrollment programs (Pérez, Cortés, Ramos, Coronado, 2010). Dual enrollment programs make it possible for students to take college courses at no cost while they attend high school.

Undocumented students should be provided with information and guidance through the college preparation, application, and college-going processes. Due to the cumbersome nature of the college and scholarship application processes, undocumented students require a great deal of individualized support. As such, the support and information they receive at school plays a large role in determining whether or not they successfully apply to college and secure financial assistance. Because undocumented students are often not expected to attend college and are less likely to come from families that possess the necessary college knowledge, the guidance they receive from teachers and counselors is particularly crucial. When undocumented students receive timely and accurate information about their postsecondary options, they are much more likely to prepare for, apply to, and persist through college (Oliverez, 2007).

Student affairs professionals should expand their outreach and recruitment beyond the traditional mechanisms of college fairs, campus visits, and high school visits. These efforts should include directly seeking out students instead of expecting the students to come to them. Because the undocumented students may be fearful to seek out information, it is imperative that they are made aware of the institutions and individuals that can provide them with support and greater opportunity. In schools with significant immigrant student populations, information regarding the naturalization process, opportunities for legal employment, higher education opportunities, and funding for college should be made available. Outreach for undocumented students should also encompass a consistent and long-standing presence in the community to include schools and culturally relevant community locations (Gildersleeve & Ranero, 2010). Furthermore, student affairs practitioners working in college admissions should be prepared to answer questions that are relevant to undocumented students, such as how their immigration status will affect their admission and the funding of their education. In developing these outreach and recruitment efforts, it is important to take into account the unique context and challenges of each community in order to more effectively engage in the work required to increase undocumented student access to higher education.

It is also important to consider that many undocumented students are also first-generation college students. In general, first-generation students select institutions based on the availability of financial aid, proximity to home, and their ability to work while enrolled (Nuñez & Carroll, 1998). Given that undocumented students are often first-generation college students, student affairs practitioners should be aware that time, educational goals, and planning may take on different meanings and values for them. Many first-generation undocumented college students feel conflicted between their own desires to pursue postsecondary education with their sense of duty to be an integral part of their family structures (London, 1989). Given these and other dynamics, student affairs practitioners must be willing to engage in approaches that require them to take multiple factors into consideration to ensure that undocumented students succeed.

Informed Advice while Protecting Student Confidentiality

Identifying an undocumented student on a college campus is not possible at first glance, thus it is critical to be sensitive when a student chooses to disclose their delicate secret. Undocumented students look like their peers and may be found in residence halls, student unions, classrooms, and student organizations. It is a self-disclosed identity that a student must feel comfortable sharing. Students often decide to share their secrets with individuals they trust that can provide honest, direct, and informed advice while protecting their confidentiality (Hernandez, Hernandez, & Gadson et al., 2010). Therefore, it also is important for faculty and staff to identify ways to create opportunities for students to feel comfortable disclosing. Faculty and staff cannot serve students well when they are not aware of the circumstances and challenges that undocumented students face in their pursuit of higher education. The fear that college personnel will not be receptive and empathetic to their status can result in students' unwillingness to trust educators when asked to reveal significant impediments to their educational experience (Hernandez, Hernandez, & Gadson et al., 2010).

Support Financing Higher Education

The financial difficulties that undocumented students encounter are among the most difficult obstacle to overcome. Indeed, when asked about their greatest challenge in pursuing higher education, both students and those who work with them contend that undocumented students' ineligibility for financial aid combined with their families' limited financial means are most prohibitive (Oliverez, 2006). Even in states like California, where in-state tuition policies make college more affordable for undocumented students, many of them are still unable to afford higher education. Schools at every level need to develop a strategic plan for systematically raising funds to support undocumented students who wish to attend college.

Increasingly, high school teachers, counselors, and a variety of higher education professionals are helping undocumented students fundraise for college (Oliverez, 2007). In California, some community college faculty have already developed special committees to help raise money for students. Some of these efforts include faculty and staff automatic monthly payroll deductions that are transferred to a fund for undocumented student scholarships (see Pérez, Cortés, Ramos, & Coronado, 2010). Still, there is more that can be done. Schools with access to private funds or the ability to solicit private funds can work together with local organizations and businesses to develop scholarships specifically for undocumented students. This is of particular importance because much of the money available through public institutions is considered government funds, and therefore, are unavailable to undocumented students. In instances when private funds are available, undocumented students are sometimes able to receive financial support. Some private scholarship providers also deem undocumented students ineligible for their awards. Advocacy can play an important role in making these funds available to undocumented students. Many scholarship providers are unaware of the challenges to college access that undocumented students encounter. School- and college-based professionals can work with groups and individuals in their area who provide financial support to college students to make sure they understand why extending this aid to undocumented students is crucial. This type of advocacy could lead to greater funds being made available to undocumented students on their campuses. If schools form partnerships with the intent of soliciting or developing scholarship funds for undocumented students, their efforts could play a critical role in providing these students with greater financial access to higher education. This would also make students and families more confident that financial support would be available if and when the students reach higher education. Although, nationwide, community colleges have been slow to take on fundraising efforts (Lanning, 2008; Romano, Gallagher, & Shugart, 2010), foundation dollars can be used strategically to meet the needs of students who cannot qualify for federal aid such as undocumented students. Romano, Gallagher, and Shugart (2010), for example, describe a collaboration between a community college's student affairs leaders and a foundation that resulted in raising $3 million for a private scholarship fund.

In becoming familiar with their local law and policy, student affairs professionals should pay particular attention to admission, tuition, and financial aid policies at their institutional and state levels. Recognizing that some laws and policies may afford undocumented students greater opportunity (i.e., in-state tuition benefits), while others may constrain students' opportunity (i.e., restrictive financial aid policies), student affairs professionals can assess their immediate situations and explore creative ways to assist students. Understanding that undocumented students may struggle to afford college yet may not qualify for financial aid, student affairs professionals may find opportunities for students to work in situations where compensation can come in forms that may not require reporting to federal agencies, such as smaller stipends for special projects or service (Gildersleeve, Rumann, & Mondragon, 2010).

Advocacy

One of the best ways student affairs professionals can serve undocumented students, from a legal and policy perspective, is to become advocates for students. Advocacy means going beyond the basic service of informing oneself about the local law and policy, but demonstrating to undocumented students the importance of struggling in their quest for educational opportunity. Supporting and engaging in activities such as letter-writing campaigns in support of beneficial legislation provide evidence to undocumented students that student affairs professionals desire to support them in their lives as college students. Advocacy is central to student affairs work, and it should not be restricted to students' lives on campus. Rather, advocacy should work to benefit students on campus by recognizing ways that the legal and policy contexts off-campus shape students' lives in college (Pérez, Munoz, Alcantar, Guarneros, In Press).

Community college administrators can also work to build coalitions with grassroots and community-based organizations (CBO's) that normally advocate for the rights of immigrants and youth community development. Creating an alliance to form a common interest (e.g., improving conditions for undocumented families) can make a great difference system-wide. Collaboration with CBO's that work closely with community members and political officials to improve the educational access of undocumented students in community colleges could focus on passing in-state tuition legislation in states that currently do not.

The principles of social justice counseling can be used to guide efforts to support undocumented students. Counseling professionals are gradually changing their method of practice and training to effectively meet the needs of underserved student populations by adopting the social justice counseling paradigm as a holistic approach to addressing the social and educational inequities that low-income minority youth frequently experience in their educational institutions and communities (Lee, 2005). These efforts involve addressing issues such as poverty, pollution, health care access, street violence, and institutional racism through psychoeducational workshops and conferences in order to promote awareness and advocacy.

Student Groups

Undocumented-student organizations are also critically important sources of support for college students. Recognizing the general lack of information among families and even school officials about the rights that undocumented students has prompted the development of student-led college groups that provide information about higher education access to students, parents, teachers and counselors. In California, student information sharing and advocacy within higher education settings are moving an increasing number of students through California's public college and university system being less dependent on the actions of front-line workers by drawing on the resources in their student networks (Chavez et al., 2007; Gonzales, 2008). A perfect example of undocumented student-led efforts is UCLA IDEAS (Improving Dreams Equality, Access, and Success), an organization that has pioneered student initiated recruitment and retention strategies that take into account the precollege contexts of undocumented students (Escobar, Lozano, & Inzunza, 2008). With similar groups spread across campuses in California, IDEAS draws on the wealth of assets that current and previous undocumented students share from their actual experiences as well as academic research, institutional resources, and the participation of other student and educator allies. By centering on the social contexts of undocumented students' precollege lives, IDEAS' workshops and practices manage to support students and meet them where they are, validating their struggles to persist through education as undocumented students (Gildersleeve & Ranero, 2010).

Improving Career Development for Undocumented Students

Although internships may not lead directly to paid employment for undocumented students, they offer excellent potential for building much-needed allies and networks that will help them secure positions and desired legal employment sponsorship (Ortiz & Hinojosa, 2010).
Because networks are invaluable to undocumented students, the identification of role models and mentors is a needed component in the career development process. At times this is difficult because the role model relationship tends to be established more easily when mentor and mentee share a common ethnic or racial background (Karunanayake & Nauta, 2004). In some fields or industries, finding these mentors is a challenge, especially with the compounded element of immigration status. The secrecy involved with being undocumented, and in disclosing previous undocumented status, makes finding a match an arduous process. In addition, students may assume that professionals or faculty who share their ethnic background will be sensitive to their situation, but they may find that some support more

restrictive immigration policies. Career center staff should work diligently to include allies for undocumented students in their professional networks so that they can refer students to professionals who are willing to help them navigate any barriers (Ortiz & Hinojosa, 2010). The use of "safe zones," similar to those offered to lesbian, gay, bisexual, and transgender students, may also be a positive strategy to help undocumented students find appropriate and welcoming career mentors (Ortiz & Hinojosa, 2010).

Some college career centers are developing specialized services for undocumented students, often initiated by individual staff and faculty members who work outside their typical job responsibilities to reach out to undocumented students. In California, progressive career centers on campuses with larger numbers of undocumented students support and encourage professional development activities to help career counselors and other career center personnel become well versed in the needs of undocumented students and to learn how to customize services and opportunities to meet their needs (Ortiz& Hinojosa, 2010). Often, career center staff become expert problem solvers and troubleshooters for undocumented students, and are open to brainstorming with students to help them to developing alternative solutions.

Creating a Welcoming and Supportive Campus Environment

Institutions need to create welcoming and supportive environments for undocumented students to facilitate their full integration into campus life. Students who can access campus resources have more opportunities to develop personal and professional skills that can outweigh the risk of jeopardizing their identity. Creating campus environments that foster and promote students' growth is of the utmost importance, yet for undocumented students, these opportunities may be limited. One of the ways community colleges can accomplish this goal is by establishing multicultural support programs where staff can play a role in affirming cultural pride, hope, and dignity with students (Herr, 2004). Students with anxiety and fear are more likely to go where they sense comfort and ease (Dozier, 1993). It may also encourage skeptical students to gradually open up to culturally sensitive support staff about their personal issues, especially Latino undocumented males, who are more likely to have difficulty trusting school personnel with their closely guarded secrets. Overall, undocumented students need institutional support agents who can be sensitive and empathetic to their needs. Hiring bilingual and ethnically diverse faculty and staff may also promote immigrant student engagement and foster validation (Rendón, 1994).

Health and Clinically-Oriented Services

It is essential that school psychologists and counselors receive thorough training on the socioemotional experiences of undocumented students (Dozier, 1993). These students may need help and advice on how to manage the demanding pressures of home, work, and school. Although all college students deal with such issues, many undocumented students work long hours to pay for college and personal expenses, and may suffer from anxiety, fear, and as a consequence, are likely to develop physiological problems (Potochnik & Perreira, 2010). Some may still harbor anguish and resentment toward their parents, peers, and may not know how to deal effectively with such emotions. Many students are in danger of dropping out if an effective support system is not in place. As such, colleges that serve large numbers of undocumented students are urged to invest in more specialized, cross-culturally sensitive psychologists and therapists that are adequately trained for working with issues related to undocumented status. Psychoeducational workshops focusing on anxiety, alienation, depression, stress management, and post-traumautic stress disorder are just some of the services that can be made available to undocumented students.

Past research has mostly focused on the educational, sociohistorical, and psychological challenges of immigrant and ethnic minority populations. This study is one of the few that has specifically examined the socioemotional functioning of undocumented Latino college students. By addressing the major obstacles to college access for undocumented students described in this section, high schools and colleges can not only help reduce student distress and anxiety, but also eliminate many of the barriers that currently prevent these students from applying to, getting admitted to, and persisting in higher education. By taking steps like partnering to provide professional development, systematically disseminating relevant information to undocumented students and their families, and soliciting scholarship funds to provide financial support to undocumented students, educational institutions can help to facilitate greater access to higher education for this vulnerable population.

CHAPTER 6
Conclusion

Our findings highlight that most undocumented Latino students attending community colleges experience a variety of socioemotional and academic challenges. They frequently struggle with feelings of shame, trepidation, anger, despair, marginalization, and uncertainty. These socially driven emotions are often derived from experiences of discrimination, anti-immigrant sentiment, fear of deportation, and systemic barriers (e.g., ineligibility for college financial assistance). Chapter 3 notes that although these students dedicate themselves to school and doing well academically, they soon learn that opportunities promised them, as a result of their academic success, preclude them. Despite meeting the eligibility criteria, undocumented students are not able to participate in a variety of programs that require proof of legal status such as internships, study abroad programs, academic enrichment programs, and scholarships. Although their academic credentials make them eligible for such programs, their status prevents them from being able to reap the rewards of their educational investments. At the college level, they are ineligible for any form of public funding and must work long hours to afford the cost of tuition. Since they are not eligible to apply for a driver's license, they depend on unreliable public transportation to get to school. These daily challenges are constant reminders of the numerous limitations they face due to their legal status.

Additionally, students see their U.S.-born classmates, who despite inferior academic records, are able to pursue a college education having access to full financial resources not available to them. Despite moments of despair, undocumented students find ways to reframe their circumstances in positive terms (Farley et al., 2005). They also compare their circumstances with conditions in their country of origin, with those around them who are less fortunate, or peers who had made bad life decisions (Suarez-Orozco & Suarez-Orozco, 1995). They contrast their limited opportunities with what was available in their country of origin and use that perspective to remain committed to their educational goals. Many frequently remind themselves how much harder their lives would be if they had made the same poor decisions as some of their peers (e.g., pregnancy, gangs, dropping out of high school). Students' parents also encouraged them by using similar methods, such as taking them to their physically-demanding, low-wage jobs to see what their occupational future might look like if they do not pursue higher education.

Older undocumented college students also serve as positive role models. Study participants often interacted with other undocumented Latino students who had been able to earn four-year college and graduate degrees who encouraged them to continue with higher education studies, despite the challenges. Although they face an uncertain future, rather than become dejected, some students reframed their situation and were driven to succeed. Others felt an additional need to prove to individuals with anti-immigrant views that they are more than capable of making positive contributions to society.

Another source of motivation for undocumented students was their sense of obligation to their parents. Many felt a genuine sense of appreciation for the sacrifices their parents had made to bring them to the U.S. for a better life. Even at the prospect of earning a college degree, and not being able to use it, community college students highlight the sense of accomplishment from just becoming "educated," regardless of their employment options in the future because they want to make their parents proud and see it as a way to repay their parents for all the sacrifices they have made for them.

The results of our research are consistent with Dozier's (1995) findings on undocumented community college students. She found that one of the primary motivators for undocumented students is to acquire the education necessary to realize their professional aspirations and become economic contributors in this country. The study also revealed students' academic resilience and the important role of strong support networks. Supportive teachers, counselors, and parents often play a key role in helping students maintain a positive outlook. Participants who actively sought and received academic and social support from college faculty, student services personnel, and peers fared better (Stanton-Salazar, 2001). Some students were able to access academic outreach programs such as AVID, Puente, SHPE, and MESA, while others sought support from student clubs, community-based organizations, and other programs that did not require citizenship information in order to participate.

Chapter 4 demonstrates that in addition to their after school jobs, responsibilities at home, and volunteer work, undocumented students are involved in sports, student council, band, and the school newspaper. Once students reach college, however, their increasing work hours to pay for tuition costs negatively impact their extracurricular participation rates. This is a remarkable finding given the numerous obstacles undocumented students face due to their legal status, including working long hours per week to pay for school and personal expenses, and in many cases, difficulty finding reliable transportation to their volunteer activities.

Although not always their first choice, most college-eligible undocumented students enroll at their local community college. These institutions often serve as their de facto gateway to higher education due to their low cost and close proximity to their homes. At the community college, students frequently find supportive and nurturing faculty and enroll in academic outreach programs which provide rigorous academic courses that are important sources of information on how to transfer to a four-year university. The community college experience, however, is not without its tribulations. Even with low-tuition rates, students still struggle to make their tuition payments and balance school with long hours working at minimum-wage jobs. Many students are forced to take frequent leaves of absence from college due to a lack of money, prolonging their stay at the community college. Although some students are fortunate to attend community colleges that provide various forms of support, others are not so lucky as some community colleges have no idea undocumented students are a part of their student body and thus have no resources in place to help them.

The findings also indicate that young women are more likely to actively seek support and share their legal status identity with school and community agents to enlist support. These actions often result in successful access to the resources of teachers, counselors, and other school agents. Males, on other hand, were not as forthcoming in revealing their status, and subsequently, are less likely to receive the same type of support. Many felt a need to be discrete for fear of being negatively labeled or further marginalized. In addition to strategic disclosure of their status to recruit support, females are more likely than their male counterparts to attribute their academic success to a self-described trait of "stubbornness." Female students often have to contend with gender biases as well as more restrictions and responsibilities at home compared to their male siblings (Suarez-Orozco & Suarez-Orozco, 2001). As such, female participants, felt compelled to prove to pessimists or "machismo"-minded individuals that they are worthy and capable of achieving academically.

Overall, both females and males experience similar levels of discrimination, depression, and social rejection. Students report being followed at stores or supermarkets and shunned at food or night club establishments. Undocumented students also contend with regular challenges such as the inability to legally drive or apply for federal financial aid and scholarships. As a result, many develop deep feelings of rejection, and at times, resent their U.S. citizen or legalized Latino peers who they often view as not taking advantage of the resources that they desperately need.

Comparisons of three student groups with different achievement profiles (average GPA, above average GPA, and high GPA), found that the sociomotional conditions and personal characteristics of all three GPA groups did not vary significantly. The above average GPA group did report higher incidents of discrimination and uneasiness. It is possible that these students are more driven to succeed as a result of these negative experiences—which is consistent with the overall positive reframing findings. In addition, the average GPA group consisted of young parents, and those who worked very long hours, which may help explain why their academic performance was lower than the other groups. It is possible that the added responsibilities of parenting and working full-time negatively affected their academic performance. Further, the average GPA group often lamented about not having enough time to participate in extracurricular and campus activities.

Conclusion

The results from this study coincide with several studies that have documented the "immigrant paradox," which posits that first-generation immigrants have better health and educational outcomes than individuals born in the United States, despite similarly disadvantaged circumstances (Fuligni, 1997; Hummer, Powers, Pullum, Gossman, & Frisbie, 2007; Kao, 1999; Kao & Tienda, 1995; Palloni & Morenoff, 2001; Portes, 1995; Portes & Rumbaut, 1990). Explanations for this immigrant advantage include selection bias—individuals with greater psychological and physical robustness may be more likely to embark on the immigrant journey, social and kinship networks (Palloni & Morenoff, 2001), cultural norms and values transported from the home country, as well as the interplay between immigrants' characteristics and the context of reception within the United States (Portes, 1995).

These studies also suggest that immigrant youth appear to have a more optimistic view of succeeding in U.S. society, and have been shown to have greater academic motivation than their U.S. born counterparts (Frome & Eccles, 1998; Kao & Tienda, 1995; Ogbu & Simmons, 1998; Suarez-Orozco, C. & Suarez-Orozco, M., 1995). A study of the effects of the attitudes and behaviors of immigrant children and their families on academic achievement found that even after controlling for ethnicity, immigrant students emphasized educational success more than native-born peers (Fuligni, 1997). Family is often cited as having an indirect role in students' academic motivation. Some immigrant groups tend to have a stronger sense of family obligation and responsibility that may motivate them academically (Berry, Phinney, Sam, & Vedder, 2006; Fuligni, 1997). Immigrant children are also more likely than children from non-immigrant families to have parents who are married which can provide greater overall stability and parental support for development (Brandon, 2002; Leventhal et al., 2006).

Qualitative research has shown that Mexican immigrant parents place primary importance on raising children that are ''bien educado'' (well-behaved) (Valdes, 1996). These parents place great emphasis on children's respect of authority figures which may promote increased adherence to classroom rules and more respectful behavior toward teachers (Keefe & Padilla, 1987). These parental values are communicated to youth directly and are likely to influence specific parenting behaviors that support these socialization goals. Resilience and self-affirmation may also play a central role as those in the first generation may be more likely to draw on the inoculating effects of the dual frame of reference between the country of origin and the new setting ("my life is much better here than there") as well as hope (Suárez-Orozco & Suárez-Orozco, 1995; Suárez-Orozco & Suárez-Orozco, 2001).

Overall, the findings suggest that community college Latino undocumented students have a healthy socioemotional functioning despite the systemic barriers that they encounter on a daily basis. Most students have managed to overcome various barriers by actively seeking support from their families and institutional and community agents. The students' high levels of determination, expectations, self-worth, self-efficacy, and passion may help them persevere academically despite the odds against them. All of the participants in this study employed various coping mechanisms in an effort to counteract negative experiences associated with their undocumented, low-income minority status. Participants received help from their parents, empathetic teachers, counselors, and community members. These protective factors, helped students maintain their optimism and motivation to succeed in spite of institutional discrimination and living with uncertainty, a finding consistent with previous findings (Borman & Overman, 2004; Wang et al., 1994). Unfortunately, out of the estimated 65,000 undocumented high school students that graduate every year, few are fortunate enough to find the necessary support to continue with higher education studies (Johnston, 2000a). We still need research that focuses on students who do not persist after high school. Although financial restrictions are significant, there may be other important factors yet uncovered.

Although our study provides important insights into the educational experiences of undocumented community college Latino students, results should not be over generalized. The small sample of 37 community college participants may not be representative of this population who attend community colleges nationwide. It is also important to note that we only had a few male participants which may be due to the underrepresentation of Latino males in higher education generally (Kewal Ramani, Gilbertson, Fox, & Provasnik, 2007). Another plausible reason may be the unwillingness of males to reveal their legal status as delineated in the findings. Despite these limitations, results provide important insights on the challenges that undocumented students face and highlight important implications for institutional support and practice.

Expanding Higher Education Access for Undocumented Students

Among the eleven states that provide in-state tuition rights to undocumented students, there is a need to ensure institutional adherence to state laws, through audits of the implementation of these laws (Contreras, 2009). Many secondary and postsecondary staff in educational institutions are not fully aware of the state's in-state tuition laws. Many institutional officials are unaware of the in-state tuition laws and, as a result, did not know that undocumented students could attend college. Students are often given misinformation in high school that continues into community college and university contexts (Gonzales, 2008). Previous studies also reveal that not all college staff are willing to provide information to undocumented students (Contreras, 2009; Gonzales, 2008). Some have political differences with the current laws that provide access to admission and in-state tuition. These staff either behave in a discriminatory manner or discourage undocumented students from finding the answers they need regarding financial aid, programs or courses, thus undermining their higher education access.

The pervasive anti-immigrant climate in the nation today highlights the need for greater oversight in all institutions to ensure that Latino students in K-12 and higher education receive proper information about all the educational options available to undocumented Latino students. Previous findings strongly suggest that professional development is needed for college and university staff who routinely conduct outreach, recruitment, and work in critical offices dealing directly with undocumented students. Moreover, it is important to devise early intervention strategies that target undocumented students and their families to provide them with important information and resources. Without networks of information, many of these students miss existing opportunities. These interventions may prevent adults from discouraging undocumented students from realizing their dreams or giving them inaccurate information. Furthermore, routine audits by state entities or oversight from state Offices for Civil Rights would help ensure that in-state tuition laws are fully implemented (Contreras, 2009).

Although the eleven states that have passed laws to extend resident tuition to undocumented students are clearly attempting to improve their postsecondary opportunities, such laws do not address the limitations inherent in having undocumented status. For example, they do not remedy the fact that under current federal law undocumented students are not eligible for any of the $199 billion distributed annually in federal financial aid, work study, and loans for postsecondary education (Baum, Payea, Cardenas-Elliott, 2010). The lack of access to federal funds for postsecondary education represents a financial barrier to college for undocumented students that even resident tuition cannot offset. For example, over the last five years, the average advertised tuition and fees at U.S. public institutions has increased 40 percent at four-year institutions, and 19 percent at two-year institutions. For the lowest-income families, such sharp increases mean that without access to student aid, the average price of public four-year colleges and universities would comprise nearly 29 percent of their total household income and the price of two-year institutions would make up about 11 percent. Because undocumented students are not eligible for federal financial aid and in all but two cases are not eligible for state aid, even with in-state tuition rates, college—particularly four-year institutions—may still be out of reach. Thus, while many lower-income, undocumented students have high expectations that they will attend college, these expectations do not match reality (Hearn, 2001). For example, a 2003 study of the undocumented and legal immigrant high school population in Chicago found that while more undocumented students surveyed had college aspirations (80 percent) than did their legal immigrant counterparts (77 percent), 43 percent of undocumented students indicated that they did not know how they would pay for college, compared to 17 percent of immigrant students with legal status (Mehta & Ali, 2003).

Expanding the Undocumented Student Educational Pipeline

While it's important to implement institutional practices to support undocumented students currently enrolled in higher education, it's equally important to increase access to the vast majority of students that never enter higher education. Focusing primarily on the experiences of undocumented university students, researchers have documented their struggles on college campuses (Contreras, 2009; Pérez-Huber & Malagon, 2007), academic resilience (Pérez, Espinoza, Ramos, Coronado, & Cortés, 2009), and civic activity (Abrego, 2008; Gonzales, 2008; Pérez, Espinoza, Ramos, Coronado, & Cortés, 2010; Rincón, 2008; Rogers, Saunders, Terriquez, & Velez, 2008). Although this important research has uncovered important findings about a relatively little-known population, what we know about this population draws narrowly from the experiences of undocumented students on college and university campuses. Very little is known about their educational experiences in K-12 settings.

Access to higher education for undocumented students is extremely difficult for a variety of reasons. Nationally, among undocumented young adults between the ages 18 to 24, 40% have not completed high school, and among high school graduates, only 49% are in college or have attended college (Passel & Cohn, 2009). Although undocumented youths who arrive in the United States before the age of 14 fare slightly better—72% finish high school and 61% of high school graduates go on to college—these figures are still much lower than for U.S.-born residents. Given the poverty profile of most undocumented families, undocumented children often grow up in cramped, overcrowded dwellings in increasingly segregated neighborhoods. This places them in large school districts and at schools with high student-to-teacher ratios. With limited access to teachers and counselors, many students quickly fall through the cracks.

Gonzales (2010) argues that tracking plays a central role in the lack of higher education access for undocumented students. In his study, he found that positively tracked students were put into special programs as early as seventh grade. Thus, by the time they reach high school, they are prepared to transition into the gifted and talented programs, specialized academies, and Honors/AP classes. Identified as high achievers and "smart kids," their positive labels are reinforced, giving them the affirmation needed to continue their academic success. Their experiences illustrate that positive tracking and close relationships with school personnel mediate some of the negative effects of undocumented status, by providing positively tracked undocumented students important access to the mechanisms that facilitate college matriculation. Negatively tracked students, on the other hand, have the opposite experience. Most students in the lower ability tracking groups feel disconnected from school, do not have significant relationships with teachers, and feel negatively labeled, and shut out of many important academic support services.

Undocumented students often struggle deciding whether to conceal or reveal the details of their undocumented status. Many report feeling embarrassed to tell friends and scared of the repercussions among peers and adults. In most cases, they would rather conceal their stigma. However, higher-track students who have trusting relationships with teachers, counselors, and other mentors are more likely to disclose their status because they feel comfortable disclosing private details about their family's financial difficulties or their undocumented status to school personnel. As a result, they are able to receive more guidance and support during the college application process (Gonzales, 2010). Students in large, general track classes, on the other hand, have less individualized attention and fewer opportunities to form positive relationships with teachers and school officials. The inability to form relationships with teachers in their general track classes shuts them out of many opportunities. Without access to scarce school resources, many of these students fall through the cracks. They are not able to get help when they needed it and do not have relationships from which to draw assistance for personal and family problems. Most important, not having relationships with adults to guide them through what is probably the most important and daunting transition in their lives has potentially disastrous effects. Without special attention and support, not being able to get into college—because of dropping out, lacking the necessary information, or simply not being on track to go to college—thrusts them into an adult world where nearly every domain of day-to-day adult life is legally off-limits (Gonzales, 2010).

Improving the Well-being of All Undocumented Students

Thirty-five years ago, in 1975, the State of Texas passed a law to deny undocumented immigrant students' access to public education. In a lawsuit that reached the highest court, the Supreme Court decided in 1982 that undocumented students had the right to attend K-12

Conclusion

regardless of their immigration status, a right guaranteed by the equal protection clause of the Fourteenth Amendment. Rincón (2008) further argues for an expansion of undocumented students' educational rights to include higher education in the same way that other researchers have drawn on the precepts of equality and equity guaranteed under the U.S. constitution to argue against school practices such as academic tracking (Oakes, 1985; Rincón, 2008; Wells and Serna, 1996). In its ruling over twenty-eight years ago, the Supreme Court pointed out that "without an education, these undocumented children,"[a]lready disadvantaged as a result of poverty, lack of English speaking ability and undeniable racial prejudices...will become permanently locked into the lowest socioeconomic class" (*Plyler v. Doe*, 1982, p. 208). In this respect, the argument that the denial of education creates a permanent underclass still holds, even for high school graduates as it is widely accepted that a high school diploma is not sufficient to acquire most jobs that allow individuals to earn a "living wage."

Until now, this battle for undocumented youth has been fought almost exclusively in the realm of higher education. Growing numbers of undocumented children are moving into adulthood, while only about 5% to 10% of all undocumented high school graduates goes on to college (Passel & Cohn, 2009). In 2001, almost twenty years after the *Plyler* ruling, Texas became the first state to allow the same population of undocumented students' access to college at in-state tuition rates. As of 2010, ten other states have also passed similar laws. With few funding sources available, in-state tuition laws for undocumented students have been found to have a significant effect. Undocumented students are 1.54 times more likely to enroll in a postsecondary institution if a state offers in-state tuition rather than out-of-state tuition charge (Flores, & Horn, 2010). Undocumented students are also 69% more likely to enroll in college if they reside in a metropolitan area within a state that offers in-state tuition than one that does not (Flores & Oseguera, 2010).

As increasing numbers of undocumented students graduate from college, they remain undocumented and unable to make use of their training upon completion, highlighting the need to allow this population to adjust their immigration status. From a public policy perspective, increased educational attainment levels of undocumented immigrants are less than effective if they are not accompanied by federal legislation that provides a path to legalization to fully maximize the personal and societal benefits of their increased skills. Many of these young people aim to be public servants because their lived experiences have created a desire to give back to their communities. Until current immigration policies are reformed, these young people will continue to be unable to fulfill their aspirations and contribute to society. Without the ability to actualize their education in the legal workforce their situation represents wasted talent.

The DREAM Act

The size of the undocumented population along with its dispersal to nontraditional destinations (states other than California, Florida, Illinois, New Jersey, New York, and Texas) has made immigrant students' lack of access to higher education a national issue. The fact that states such as Kansas, Oklahoma Utah, and Washington have passed legislation to allow in-state tuition for undocumented students underscores the need for national legislation to insure nationwide college access and legalization opportunities for this population.

Olivas (2004) argues that the issue of undocumented student college admission is "alternatively, an admissions case, an immigration matter, a taxpayer suit, a state civil procedure issue, an issue of preemption, a question of higher education tuition and finance, a civil rights case, and a political issue. At bottom, though, it is a story about college-aged kids who have lived virtually all their lives in the United States and who want to attend college and enjoy the upward mobility a college degree provides" (Olivas, 1995, p.1021; 2004, p.36). In that respect while the in-state tuition laws allow these students the opportunity to obtain a post-secondary degree, current immigration federal law keeps them from being employed thus thwarting the possibility to enjoy the upward mobility conferred by their college diplomas.

The DREAM Act represents a powerful imperative for recipients of conditional status to either pursue a college education or join the military. It also provides a strong incentive for unauthorized children now in U.S. schools to finish high school, and it may provide a strong incentive to recent unauthorized dropouts to complete their schooling or obtain a GED. Making legal status conditional on young adults'

Conclusion

educational and military choices has no precedent in U.S. immigration policy. The DREAM Act does not guarantee any undocumented student the right to remain in the United States, and does not grant automatic or blanket amnesty to its potential beneficiaries. However, it does give some who have been acculturated in the United States the opportunity of earning the right to remain. The continuing neglect of immigration reform not only ignores the hardship endured by millions who live in American society as de facto second-class citizens, it also ignores the ongoing loss of thousands of talented college going undocumented students.

Like *Plyler v. Doe,* the DREAM Act is only a *partial* solution. School experiences have a strong bearing on future success or failure. As the literature on educational achievement has consistently stated, Latino students continue to lag behind their peers in educational achievement. Confronted with very large schools and inadequate resources to meet their needs, many of these students are left to fall through the cracks. In order to ensure the success of legislation such as the DREAM Act, it is of utmost importance to increase the number of potential beneficiaries. Ultimately, this means addressing existing inequalities within the school system. In order for something like the DREAM Act to have an impact, school reform needs to happen simultaneously.

The framing of immigrants as "illegal" often serves to hide our shared humanity and allows anti-immigrant sentiment, policies, and practices to become normalized ways of responding to undocumented immigration. The constructions of Latino immigrants as criminal, dangerous, and threatening to an "American" way of life reiterated in the media, saturating public discourse with negative images of Latino immigrants, reinforce the "illegal" frame. These negative portrayals of undocumented Latino immigrants have become so prevalent within immigration discourse that they have become "common sense" in how we understand immigration issues and subsequently inform institutional policies that deny undocumented immigrants the same rights and treatment as their U.S.-born and "legalized" counterparts (Chávez, 2001, 2008; Santa Ana, 2002).

To fully rectify the flaws in our ineffective immigration system, we must move beyond current over simplistic notions of "illegality." After having been educated in our schools, undocumented students speak English (often with more ease than Spanish), envision their futures here, and powerfully internalize U.S. values and expectations of merit. However, there are no available structural paths, even for those who excel academically. For most undocumented students, their birthplace was literally a "geographic accident of birth," as they were brought to the United States by their parents when they were very young, and have resided and lived in the country for virtually all their lives. Since they were raised in the United States during their formative years, they consider themselves Americans. In fact, most know no other culture other than that of the United States, as their ties with their native countries were severed years ago when they immigrated to the United States with their parents. Most students do not even become aware of their lack of legal status until their final years in high school. Without full legal rights, undocumented youth will continue to be barred from the traditional paths of upward mobility available to other immigrants throughout U.S. history.

Preventing undocumented high school graduates from obtaining higher education is bad public policy. From a social standpoint, these impediments permanently lock these immigrants into the lowest socioeconomic class, perpetuating poverty among Latino immigrant communities. As a nation, we must do the right thing when it comes to undocumented students. We demonize them, rather than see them for what they are- human beings entering for a better life who have been manipulated by globalization, regional economies, and social structures that have operated for generations. Lack of legal status renders immigrants not simply foreigners, but brands them as criminals, subject to expulsion—as no less than complete outcasts. We should welcome undocumented students who have already become part of the social fabric of our nation by facilitating access to higher education and providing a path to citizenship. Like all our immigrant predecessors, they are here to seek a better life through hard work and dedication to school, family, and community.

APPENDICES

Appendix A: Survey

Please respond to the following set of questions. Remember, there are no right or wrong answers.

1. Please list any awards you received or special activities in which you were chosen to participate during **Elementary School:**

   _____

   _____

2. Please list any extracurricular activities in which you participated during **Elementary School** (for example, band, team sports, student council, drama, Mecha, Academic decathlon, Chess club, Ballet folklórico, speech and debate, etc.).

   _____

   _____

3. Please list any leadership positions you held in **Elementary School** (for example: team captain, band chair, student council president, club officer).

   _____

   _____

4. Did you volunteer or do community service in **Elementary School** (circle one)?   Yes   No

5. If you volunteered or did community service in **Elementary School**, approximately how many hours per year did you volunteer?

6. Please list all your volunteer or community service activities during **Elementary School**:

MIDDLE SCHOOL

7. Please list any awards you received in **Middle School**:

8. Please list any extracurricular activities in which you participated during **Middle School**

9. Please list any leadership positions you held in **Middle School** (for example: team captain, band chair, student council president, club officer):

10. Please list any summer programs in which you participated during **Middle School** (for example, MESA, Upward Bound, etc.):

Appendix A

11. If you volunteered or did community service in **Middle School**, approximately how many hours per year did you volunteer?

12. Please list all your volunteer or community service activities during **Middle School**:

HIGH SCHOOL

13. Please list any awards you received in **High School**:

14. Please list any extracurricular activities in which you participated during **High School** (for example, band, team sports, student council, drama, Mecha, Academic decathlon, Chess club, Yearbook, School Newspaper, Ballet folklorico, speech and debate, etc.):

15. Please list any leadership positions you held in **High School** (for example: team captain, band chair, student council president, club officer, editor-in-chief, etc.):

16. Please list any summer programs in which you participated during **High School** (for example, MESA, Upward Bound, internship, etc.):

17. If you volunteered or did community service in **High School**, approximately how many hours per year did you volunteer?

18. Please list all your volunteer or community service activities during **High School**:

19. Did you participate in a GATE/gifted education/magnet program (circle one)? Yes   No

20. If yes, in what grade did you start GATE/gifted education/magnet program?

21. Did you attend a magnet high school or private boarding school?   Yes   No

22. What was your approximate overall GPA in High School (out of a 4.0 scale)?

23. List all the AP/Honors courses you took in high school:

24. What was your **high school class rank** (for example 3/250 students) when you graduated?

Appendix A 135

25. Please list any awards you have received in **College**:

26. Please list any extracurricular activities you have participated in **College** (for example, band, team sports, student council, drama, Mecha, Academic decathlon, Chess club, Ballet folklorico, speech and debate, school newspaper, study abroad program, etc.):

27. Please list any leadership positions you have held in **College** (for example: team captain, band chair, student council president, club officer, etc.):

28. Please list any summer programs in which you have participated during **College** (for example, research programs, internships, conferences, etc.):

29. If you have volunteered or done community service in **College**, approximately how many hours per year have you volunteered?

30. Please list all your volunteer or community service activities during **College**:

31. What is your approximate overall GPA in college (out of a 4.0 scale)? _____

32. What is your college major? _____

33. What is your current occupation/job? _____

34. How many hours per week do you work? _____

35. Did you work during high school?   Yes____ No____

36. If so, how many hours per week did you work in high school? _____

37. What was your job during high school? _____

38. If you could do exactly what you wanted, how far <u>would you like</u> to go in school? (check one)

____Some college

____Graduate from a <u>two</u>-year college with an associate's degree (AA)

____Graduate from a <u>four</u>-year college with a bachelor's degree (BA)

____Get a master's degree (MA; teaching credential, social work, business)

____Get a law degree, a Ph.D., or a medical doctor's degree

39. We can't always do what we want to do. How far do you <u>think you will</u> go in school? (check one)

____Some college

____Graduate from a <u>two</u>-year college with an associate's degree (AA)

____Graduate from a <u>four</u>-year college with a bachelor's degree (BA)

____Get a master's degree (MA; teaching credential, social work, business)

____Get a law degree, a Ph.D., or a medical doctor's degree

Appendix A

Please answer the following questions:

		Not at all						Very Much
40.	To what extent will prejudice and discrimination against others like you impose barriers to their future outcomes?	1	2	3	4	5	6	7
41.	If you do worse than you expected in your life, to what extent will this be caused by discrimination against you because of your race?	1	2	3	4	5	6	7

		Strongly Disagree						Strongly Agree
42.	In the United States, anyone from any racial group can accomplish all their dreams.	1	2	3	4	5	6	7
43.	In the United States, it is possible for people from all racial groups to get ahead.	1	2	3	4	5	6	7
44.	Other members of my racial group experience discrimination.	1	2	3	4	5	6	7
45.	Most people are prejudiced against Latinos in at least some ways.	1	2	3	4	5	6	7
46.	Being Latino(a), I will probably have to work harder than most people in order to get ahead.	1	2	3	4	5	6	7

		Not important at all		Somewhat Important				Very important
47.	For someone in your racial group, how important is a good education for getting a good job?	1	2	3	4	5	6	7
48.	For someone in your racial group, how important is a good education for having a successful career?	1	2	3	4	5	6	7

Please answer the following questions:

	Not at all important	Somewhat Important	Very Important
49. How important is it to you to earn good grades in college?	1　2	3　4　5	6　7
50. How important is it for you to go to graduate school after graduating from college?	1　2	3　4　5	6　7
51. How important is it for you to go to a top-rated graduate university after graduating from college?	1　2	3　4　5	6　7
52. How important is it for you get an "A" in all your classes?	1　2	3　4　5	6　7
53. How important is it to you to do well in school?	1　2	3　4　5	6　7

Because of my undocumented background:

	Never	Almost Never	Seldom	Sometimes	Often	Almost Always	Always
54. I feel that I am not wanted in this country.	1	2	3	4	5	6	7
55. I don't feel accepted by other Americans.	1	2	3	4	5	6	7
56. I feel that Americans have something against me.	1	2	3	4	5	6	7

Appendix A

How well do you do the following?

		Not at all	Not Very Well	Well	Very Well
57.	Understand spoken English	1	2	3	4
58.	Speak English	1	2	3	4
59.	Read English	1	2	3	4
60.	Write English	1	2	3	4
61.	Understand spoken Spanish	1	2	3	4
62.	Speak Spanish	1	2	3	4
63.	Read Spanish	1	2	3	4
64.	Write Spanish	1	2	3	4

Please answer the following questions:

		Strongly disagree						Strongly Agree
65.	Being good in school is an important part of who I am.	1	2	3	4	5	6	7
66.	Doing well on intellectual tasks is very important to me.	1	2	3	4	5	6	7
67.	Academic success is not very important to me.	1	2	3	4	5	6	7
68.	It usually doesn't matter to me one way or the other how I do in school.	1	2	3	4	5	6	7
69.	Personal advancement in American society is possible for individuals of all races.	1	2	3	4	5	6	7
70.	America is an open society where individuals of any race can achieve higher personal status.	1	2	3	4	5	6	7

Please answer the following questions:

		Strongly disagree						Strongly agree
71.	My parents made many sacrifices for me to come to the United States.							
72.	I don't think there are more opportunities to get ahead here than in my country of birth.	1	2	3	4	5	6	7
73.	I would like to return to live in my country of origin.	1	2	3	4	5	6	7
74.	If my family wanted to, we could go back to my country of origin to live permanently.	1	2	3	4	5	6	7
75.	Going back to my country of origin to live is not really an option for me.	1	2	3	4	5	6	7
76.	I plan to return to my country of origin after I get my education here in the United States because I'll have better opportunities to get ahead over there.	1	2	3	4	5	6	7
77.	If Latinos born in the United States would learn about the hard conditions in my country of origin, they would try harder in school.	1	2	3	4	5	6	7

Below you will find a series of questions regarding your experiences as a member of your racial/ethnic group. Please answer the questions below by circling the number that best describes your response.

		Never	One time	A few times	About once a month	A few times a month	Once a week or more
78.	Over your lifetime, how frequently have you felt ignored, overlooked, or not given service because of your racial/ethnic group?	1	2	3	4	5	6

Appendix A

Below you will find a series of questions regarding your experiences as a member of your racial/ethnic group. Please answer the questions below by circling the number that best describes your response.

	Never	One time	A few times	About once a month	A few times a month	Once a week or more
79. Over your lifetime, how frequently have you felt treated rudely or disrespectfully because of your racial/ethnic group?	1	2	3	4	5	6
80. Over your lifetime, how frequently have you felt accused of something or treated suspiciously because of your racial/ethnic group?	1	2	3	4	5	6
81. Over your lifetime, how frequently have you felt observed or followed while in public places because of your racial/ethnic group?	1	2	3	4	5	6
82. Over your lifetime, how frequently have you felt treated as if you were "stupid," or were "talked down to" because of your racial/ethnic group?	1	2	3	4	5	6
83. Over your lifetime, how frequently have you felt your ideas or opinions were minimized, ignored, or devalued because of your racial/ethnic group?	1	2	3	4	5	6

Below you will find a series of questions regarding your experiences as a member of your racial/ethnic group. Please answer the questions below by circling the number that best describes your response.

	Never	One time	A few times	About once a month	A few times a month	Once a week or more
84. Over your lifetime, how frequently have you overheard or been told an offensive joke or comment about your racial/ethnic group?	1	2	3	4	5	6
85. Over your lifetime, how frequently have you felt insulted, called a name, or harassed because of your racial/ethnic group?	1	2	3	4	5	6

In the last month, how often would you say you have done the following?

	Almost every day	Once or twice a week	Once in a while	Almost never	Never	NA
86. Get your brother or sister ready for school.	1	2	3	4	5	6
87. Babysitting/Childcare.	1	2	3	4	5	6
88. Work in family business.	1	2	3	4	5	6
89. Help the family with shopping.	1	2	3	4	5	6

Please answer the following questions:

	Not important	Somewhat important	Important	Very important
90. For my parents, my getting good grades in school is…	1	2	3	4

Appendix A

Please answer the following questions:

		Not important	Somewhat important	Important	Very important
91.	For my parents, my going to college after high school is...	1	2	3	4
92.	For me, finishing high school is...	1	2	3	4
93.	For my friends, getting good grades in school is...	1	2	3	4
94.	For my friends, finishing high school was...	1	2	3	4
95.	For my friends, going to college after high school is...	1	2	3	4

I want to do well in school...

		Very true	Somewhat true	Somewhat false	Very false
96.	Because I want to get ahead in life.	1	2	3	4
97.	Because that is what I am supposed to do.	1	2	3	4
98.	To make my parents happy.	1	2	3	4
99.	Because I want to help my family have a better life.	1	2	3	4
100.	My friends are serious about their school work.	1	2	3	4
101.	I can count on my friends to help me in school.	1	2	3	4
102.	My friends talk to me about college.	1	2	3	4

	Very true	Somewhat true	Somewhat false	Very false
103. I have a lot of fun with my friends at school.	1	2	3	4
104. My friends encourage me to do my best in school.	1	2	3	4

Please answer the following questions:

	Strongly Disagree		Strongly Agree
105. I'm certain I can master the skills taught in class this year.	1	2 3 4	5
106. I'm certain I can figure out how to do the most difficult class work.	1	2 3 4	5
107. I can do almost all the work in class if I don't give up.	1	2 3 4	5
108. Even if the work is hard, I can learn it.	1	2 3 4	5
109. I can do even the hardest work in my classes if I try.	1	2 3 4	5
110. I would prefer to do class work that is familiar to me, rather than new work I would have to learn how to do.	1	2 3 4	5
111. I don't like to learn a lot of new concepts in my classes.	1	2 3 4	5
112. I prefer to do work as I have always done it, rather than to try something new.	1	2 3 4	5
113. I like academic concepts that are familiar to me, rather than those I haven't thought about before.	1	2 3 4	5

Appendix A

Please answer the following questions:

		Strongly Disagree				Strongly Agree
114. I would choose class work I knew I could do, rather than work I haven't done before.		1	2	3	4	5
115. I sometimes copy answers from other students during tests.		1	2	3	4	5
116. I sometimes cheat on my class work.		1	2	3	4	5
117. I sometimes copy answers from other students when I do my class work.		1	2	3	4	5
118. I sometimes annoy the professor during class.		1	2	3	4	5
119. I sometimes get into trouble with the professor during class.		1	2	3	4	5
120. I sometimes behave in a way during class that annoys the professor.		1	2	3	4	5
121. I sometimes don't follow the professor's directions during class.		1	2	3	4	5
122. I sometimes disturb the lesson that is going on in class.		1	2	3	4	5
123. Even if I do well in school, it will not help me have the kind of life I want when I grow up.		1	2	3	4	5
124. My chances of succeeding later in life don't depend on doing well in school.		1	2	3	4	5
125. Doing well in school doesn't improve my chances of having a good life when I graduate.		1	2	3	4	5

Please answer the following questions:

	Strongly Disagree				Strongly Agree
126. Getting good grades in school won't guarantee that I will get a good job when I graduate.	1	2	3	4	5
127. Even if I am successful in school, it won't help me fulfill my dreams.	1	2	3	4	5
128. Doing well in school won't help me have a satisfying career when I graduate.	1	2	3	4	5
129. I don't like to have my parents come to school because their ideas are very different from my teachers' ideas.	1	2	3	4	5
130. I feel uncomfortable when my parents come to school, because they are different from the parents of many of my classmates.	1	2	3	4	5
131. I feel troubled because my home life and my school life are like two different worlds.	1	2	3	4	5
132. I am not comfortable talking to many of my classmates because my family is very different from theirs.	1	2	3	4	5
133. When I was growing up, I had trouble finding safe places to hang out with my friends in my neighborhood.	1	2	3	4	5

Please answer the following questions:

	Strongly Disagree				Strongly Agree
134. When I was growing up, I found it difficult to find anything worthwhile to do after school in my neighborhood.	1	2	3	4	5

Appendix A

Please answer the following questions:

	Strongly Disagree				Strongly Agree
135. When I was growing up, I could find good and useful things to do on the weekends in my neighborhood.	1	2	3	4	5
136. When I was growing up, I could find many interesting and positive things to do after school in my neighborhood.	1	2	3	4	5
137. When I was growing up, there were places I could go in my neighborhood to play outdoors and have fun.	1	2	3	4	5
138. When I was growing up, there were no places I could go in my neighborhood that were attractive and clean.	1	2	3	4	5

Lately, do you...

	Never	Sometimes	Often	All the time
139. Feel critical of others?	1	2	3	4
140. Feel annoyed too easily?	1	2	3	4
141. Not have much energy?	1	2	3	4
142. Cry easily?	1	2	3	4
143. Lose your temper too easily?	1	2	3	4
144. Feel sad?	1	2	3	4
145. Worry too much?	1	2	3	4
146. Have trouble making decisions?	1	2	3	4

Lately, do you...

	Never	Sometimes	Often	All the time
147. Feel others do not understand you?	1	2	3	4
148. Eat too much?	1	2	3	4
149. Feel that people do not like you?	1	2	3	4
150. Feel like you are not as good as other people?	1	2	3	4

Below are some things that sometimes get in the way of people in <u>college</u>. Which of these might be a problem for you?

	Not a problem	Somewhat of a problem	A serious problem
151. Difficulty learning English.	1	2	3
152. Not being able to pass college exams.	1	2	3
153. Having to help at home.	1	2	3
154. Not feeling like you belong in your school.	1	2	3
155. Feeling like school work is too hard.	1	2	3

Please answer the following questions:

	Very Much like me						Not at all like me
156. Compared to other students in my classes, I expect to do well.	1	2	3	4	5	6	7
157. I am certain that I can understand the ideas taught in my classes.	1	2	3	4	5	6	7
158. I expect to do very well in school.	1	2	3	4	5	6	7

Appendix A

	Very Much like me						Not at all like me
159. Compared to others in my classes, I think I am a good student.	1	2	3	4	5	6	7
160. I am sure I can do an excellent job on the class assignments and homework.	1	2	3	4	5	6	7
161. I think I will receive good grades in my exams.	1	2	3	4	5	6	7
162. My study skills are excellent compared with others in my classes.	1	2	3	4	5	6	7
163. Compared with other students in my classes, I think I know a great deal about the subjects I'm studying.	1	2	3	4	5	6	7
164. I know that I will be able to learn the materials for the tests and exams.	1	2	3	4	5	6	7
165. I prefer class work that is challenging so I can learn new things.	1	2	3	4	5	6	7

These are questions about you and your family. Please answer them as best you can.

166. How would you describe your current status (check one)?

____Currently Undocumented

____Used to be Undocumented —Did not benefit from IRCA or Amnesty Law

____Used to be Undocumented —Benefited from IRCA or Amnesty Law

167. I am (check one):   ___Male____Female

168. How old are you? _____

169. What year in school are you in now? _____

170. In what country were you born (circle one)?   United States   Mexico
Other: (specify) _____

171. If you were born outside of the United States, what year did you enter the United States? _____

172. How old were you when you came to the United States to live? _____

173. Did you ever go to school in your country of origin? (check one)
____Yes ____No

174. If yes, circle the <u>highest</u> grade you attended outside the U.S.

   1   2   3   4   5   6   7   8   9   10   11

175. Where was you mother born (circle one)?   United States   Mexico
Other (specify) _____

176. Where was you father born (circle one)?   United States   Mexico
Other (specify) _____

177. What is the highest grade completed by your mother? (circle one)

   1 2 3 4 5 6 7 8 9 10 11 12 13 14 15 16 17+

178. What is the highest grade completed by your father? (circle one)

   1 2 3 4 5 6 7 8 9 10 11 12 13 14 15 16 17+

179. How old is your mother? _____

180. How old is your father? _____
181. What is your mother's occupation? _____

Appendix A

182. What is your father's occupation?_____

183. Does your mother speak English? (circle one)   Yes   No

184. Does your father speak English? (circle one) Yes   No

Which parents or guardians do you live with now? (check one or write in)

____Both my mother and my father in the same house

____Only my mother

____My mother and stepfather

____Only my father

____My father and stepmother

____Some of the time in my mother's home and some in my father's

____Other relatives (aunt, uncle, grandparents, etc.)

____Guardian or foster parent who is not a relative

____No parents or guardians (I live alone or with friends)

____Other (write in) _____

185. How many brothers and sisters do you have?   _____

186. How many of them were born outside of the U.S.?   _____

187. Are you the oldest child in your family? (circle your answer)   Yes   No

188. Do you still have relatives in your country of origin?   Yes   No

Appendix B: Interview Protocol

Childhood

1. What was your childhood like?
2. What do you most remember about elementary school?
3. What do you most remember about middle school?
4. Did you participate in any activities like band, sports, clubs, and/or any extra-curricular activities during middle school? If so, how did you first become involved?
5. Tell me about any awards you have received in elementary or middle school. Is there one you are most proud of? Why?
6. In middle school who influenced you the most? Why?
7. Did you attend your local library when you were growing up? How often? How old were you when you first started going?
8. Were you "popular" in elementary or middle school? What do you think made you popular?

High School (for high school graduates, ask questions in past tense)

9. What do you most remember about high school?
10. How would you describe your high school? Why?
11. Did you participate in any activities like band, sports, clubs, and/or any extra- curricular activities during high school? If so, how did you first become involved? Did you hold any leadership positions? What was that like?
12. If you worked during high school, what was it like to work and go to school in high school?
13. Tell me about any responsibilities at home that you are/were responsible for (like chores) when you came home during high school.

14. Were you in GATE (or another type of magnet program/school)? Since when? What was that like?
15. Were you "popular" in high school? What do you think made you popular?
16. Have you ever taken any advanced courses such as Honors or AP? If so, what was that like? Who encouraged you to enroll in those?
17. Tell me about any awards you have received in high school. Is there one you are most proud of? Why?
18. Did you participate in any summer programs like internships, academic enrichment, or research programs? What was that like?
19. Do you think you differ from other kids your age, living in your neighborhood?
20. What role have your parents played in your educational goals?
21. In high school, who influenced you the most? Why?
22. What role did religion play in your life when you were growing up?
23. How many people live in your house/apartment? How many bedrooms does it have?
24. Where do you study after school?
25. Any teachers who were significant to you, either positively or negatively?
26. When did you decide you wanted to go to college?

College (if applicable. If interviewee is a college graduate, ask in the past tense):

27. What do you most remember about college?
28. How would you describe your college: good college, average college, or bad college? Why?
29. Did you participate in any activities like band, sports, clubs, and/or any extra-curricular activities during college? If so, how did you first become involved? Did you hold any leadership positions? What was that like?
30. Did you participate in any summer programs like internships, academic enrichment, or research programs? What was that like?
31. If you worked during college, what was it like to work and go to school in high school?
32. In college, who influenced you the most? Why?
33. How are you paying for your college education?

Appendix B

Life for undocumented students (if not currently undocumented, ask in past tense)

34. What has it been like being an undocumented student?
35. What challenges have you encountered as an undocumented student?
36. What is the most challenging aspect of being an undocumented student?
37. Has there ever been a time when you wanted to get involved in a program or organization but couldn't because you were undocumented? Can you tell me about that?
38. Has your undocumented status made you reconsider your college plans? In what way?
39. How do you think Americans view undocumented students?
40. What is the biggest challenge you have right now?
41. Has there ever been a time when you were afraid that something would happen to you because of your undocumented status? Tell me about that.
42. Do you know of any undocumented students who are in college or who graduated from college? Have they given you any advice? How have their experiences influenced you?
43. Do you know about scholarships available to undocumented students? How did you find out?
44. How does your college experience differ from those of your U.S.-born peers?
45. Did your undocumented status influence you to apply to certain colleges and not others? Tell me about that.
46. If you were not an undocumented student, would you have applied to different colleges? Would you currently be enrolled at a different college?
47. Are there any support groups on campus for undocumented students? If so, have they been of help to you? In what ways?
48. Does your college assist undocumented students? In what way?
49. What are your occupational aspirations? What professions would you pursue if you did not have any limitations?
50. What occupation would you pursue if your current limitations continued?
51. If you were not an undocumented student, how different do you think your life would be?
52. Do you have any specific person or a group of people that you consider your support system?
53. How do you think you have contributed to society?

54. Do you think being an undocumented student has limited how much you can contribute to society? If so, how?
55. What motivates you to continue your education?
56. If you could say anything to policymakers with regard to undocumented students and educational access, what would you say?

Life after College

57. Thinking back on your educational experience so far, is there any one particular experience that you found very influential? If so, how was it influential?
58. What are your goals in life? (both educational and personal)
59. Do you want to pursue a college/graduate school education? If so, who has encouraged you to do so? (i.e., Parents, friends, teachers)
60. Tell me about your mother's involvement in activities outside the home when you were growing up (church, clubs, civic, trade unions, etc.).
61. Tell me about your father's involvement in activities outside the home when you were growing up (church, clubs, civic, trade unions, etc.).
62. Have you ever felt discriminated against or treated negatively? Tell me about those experiences.
63. How many of your friends have gone to college or plan to go to college?
64. Were you admired for any special ability when you were growing up? Tell me about that.
65. Has your physical appearance been a factor in school success? In what ways?
66. What personal characteristics that you possess were instrumental in your school success?
67. What makes you different from those students who do not get good grades and do poorly in school?
68. What one thing has contributed the most to your academic performance?
69. What significant events have played a vital role in your academic performance?
70. Were you competitive with other students in classes in high school and/or college? Why?
71. Is there anything that I didn't ask you about that you would like to share with me or that you think it would be important for me to know?

Appendix C: Scales

Academic Self-Concept (2 items)

Being good in school is an important part of who I am.
Doing well on intellectual tasks is very important to me.

Academic Self-Efficacy Scale (8 items)

I'm certain I can master the skills taught in class this year.
I'm certain I can figure out how to do the most difficult class work.
I can do almost all the work in class if I don't give up.
Even if the work is hard, I can learn it.
I can do even the hardest work in my classes if I try.

Depression (11-items)

Lately, do you...
Feel Critical of others?
Feel annoyed too easily?
Not have much energy?
Cry easily?
Lose your temper easily?
Worry too much?
Have trouble making decisions?
Feel others do not understand you?
Eat too much?
Feel people do not like you?
Feel like you are not as good as other people?

Discrimination (8-items)

Over your lifetime...
How frequently have you felt ignored, overlooked, or not given service because of your racial/ethnic group?
How frequently have you felt treated rudely or disrespectfully because of your racial/ethnic group?
How frequently have you felt accused of something or treated suspiciously because of your racial/ethnic group?
How frequently have you felt observed or followed while in public places because of your racial/ethnic group?
How frequently have you felt treated as if you were 'stupid,' or were 'talked down to' because of your racial/ethnic group?
How frequently have you felt your ideas or opinions were minimized, ignored, or devalued because of your racial/ethnic group?
How frequently have you overheard or been told an offensive joke or comment about your racial/ethnic group?
How frequently have you felt insulted, been called a name, or harassed because of your racial/ethnic group?

(School-Based) Discrimination (4-items)

How often do the following people treat you unfairly or negatively because of your racial background?—Teachers
How often do the following people treat you unfairly or negatively because of your racial background?—Counselor
How often do the following people treat you unfairly or negatively because of your racial background?—Other students
How often do the following people treat you unfairly or negatively because of your racial background?—Other adults outside school

Effort Avoidance (2-items)

I would prefer to do class work that is familiar to me, rather than new work I would have to learn how to do.
I prefer to do work as I have always done it, rather than trying something new.

Appendix C

Parent-based Motivation (2-items)

I want to do well in school...
To make my parents happy.
Because I want to help my family have a better life.

Parental Valuing of School (2 items)

For my parents, my getting good grades in school is (very important—not at all important).
For my parents, my going to college after high school is (very important—not at all important).

Rejection due to Legal Status (3 items)

Because of my AB 540 background, I feel that I am not wanted in this country.
Because of my AB 540 background, I don't feel accepted by other Americans.
Because of my AB 540 background, I feel that Americans have something against me.

Valuing of School (2 items)

How important is it to you to earn good grades?
How important is it to you to do well in school?

References

Abrego, L. J. (2006). "I can't go to college because I don't have papers": Incorporation Patterns of Latino Undocumented Youth, *Latino Studies*, 4(3): 212-231.

Abrego, L. J. (2008). Legitimacy, social Identity, and the mobilization of law: The effects of Assembly Bill 540 on undocumented students in California. *Law & Social Inquiry, 33*(3), 709–734.

Allen, K. (2006). Handout or helping hand? College scholarships for undocumented students come under fire as some corporations retract awards. *Diverse Issues in Higher Education, 23*(11), 16–17.

Allison, K.W. & Takei,Y. (1993). Diversity: The cultural contexts of adolescents and their families. In R. M. Lerner (Ed.), Early Adolescence: Perspectives on Research, Policy and Intervention. Hillsdale, NJ: Lawrence Erlbaum.

American Federation of Teachers (2008). A dream act deferred. *On Campus, 27*(3), 6.

Araujo, B., & Borrell, L. (2006). Understanding the link between discrimination, life chances, and mental health outcomes among Latino/as. *Hispanic Journal of Behavioral Sciences, 28*(2), 245–266.

Arbona, C., Olvera, N., Rodriguez, N., Hagan, J., Linares, A., & Wiesner, M. (2010). Acculturative stress among documented and undocumented Latino immigrants in the United States. *Hispanic Journal of Behavioral Sciences, 32*(3), 362-384.

Arias, A. A. (1981). *Undocumented Mexican: A study in the social psychology of clandestine migration to the United States.* Unpublished doctoral dissertation: University of California, San Diego.

Badger, E., Ericksen, B., & Yale-Loehr, S. (2000). Betwixt and between:

Undocumented aliens and access to U.S. higher education. *International Educator, IX*(4), 22-28.

Bandura, A. (2001). Social cognitive theory: An agentic perspective. *Annual Review of Psychology,* 52, 1–26.

Barry, R., & Barry, P. (1992). Establishing equality in the articulation process. In B. W. Dziech & W. R. Vilter (Eds.), *Prisoners of elitism: The community college's struggle for stature.* New Directions for Community Colleges, No. 78, No. 2, pp. 35–44). San Francisco: Jossey-Bass.

Bauer, P. F. (1994). The community college as an academic bridge. *College and University,* 69(3), 116–122.

Bailey, T. & Weininger, E.B. (2002). Performance, Graduation, and Transfer of Immigrants and Natives in City University of New York Community Colleges. *Educational Evaluation and Policy Analysis, 24, (4), 359-377.*

Bean, J. P., & Eaton, S. B. (2000). A psychological model of college student retention. In J. M. Braxton (Ed.), *Reworking the student departure puzzle.* Nashville, TN: Vanderbilt University Press.

Bean, J. P., & Metzner, B. S. (1985). Interaction effects based on class level in an explanatory model of college student dropout syndrome. *American Educational Research Journal,* 22, 35-64.

Becker, B.E. & Luthar, S. S. (2002). Social-emotional factors affecting achievement outcomes among disadvantaged students: Closing the achievement gap. *Educational Psychologist,* 37(4), 197-214.

Berk, M. L., & Schur, C. L., (2001). The effect of fear on access to care among undocumented Latino immigrants. *Journal of Immigrant Health,* 3(3), 151-156.

Bernstein, A. (1986). The devaluation of transfer: Current explanations and possible causes. In S. Zwerling (Ed.), *The community colleges and its critics.* New Directions for Community Colleges, No. 54 (pp. 31–40). San Francisco: Jossey-Bass.

Berry, J. (1990). Acculturation and adaptation: A general framework. In W. H. Holtzman and T. H. Borneman (Eds.), *The mental health of immigrants and refugees.* Austin, TX: Hogg Foundation for Mental Health, University of Texas.

Berry, J.W., Phinney, J.S., Sam, D.L., & Vedder, P. (2006). *Immigrant youth in cultural transition.* Mahwah, NJ: Erlbaum.

Bohrman, R., & Murakawa, N. (2005). Remaking big government: Immigration and crime control in the United States. In J. Sudbury (Ed.),

Global lockdown: Gender, race, and the rise of the prison industrial complex. New York, NY: Routledge.

Borglum, K., & Kubala, T. (2000). Academic and social integration of community college students: A case study. *Community College Journal of Research & Practice 24*(7), 567–577.

Borman, G.D. & Overman, L.T. (2004). Academic resilience in mathematics among poor and minority students. *The Elementary School Journal, 10*(3), 177-195.

Bragg, D. D. (2001). Community college access, mission, and outcomes: Considering intriguing intersections, and challenges. *Peabody Journal of Education, 76*(1), 93–116.

Brandon, P. D. (2002). The Living Arrangements of Children in Immigrant Families in the United States, *International Migration Review*, 36(2).

Brettell, C. B., & Sargent, C. F. (2006). Migration, identity, and citizenship: Anthropological perspectives. *American Behavioral Scientist, 50*(3), 3–8.

Brilliant, J. J. (2000). Issues in counseling immigrant college students. *Community College Journal of Research and Practice, 24*, 577–586.

Brint, S., & Karabel, J. (1989). *The diverted dream: Community colleges and the promise of educational opportunity in America, 1900–1985*. New York: Oxford University Press.

Bronfennbrenner, U. (1979). *The ecology of human development*. Cambridge, MA: Harvard University Press.

Burnam, M. A., Hough, R. L., Karno, M., Escobar, J. I., & Telles, C. A. (1987). Acculturation and lifetime prevalence of psychiatric disorders among Mexican Americans in Los Angeles. *Journal of Health & Social Behavior, 28*(1), 89–102.

Burton, L., Obeidallah, D. A., & Allison, K. (1996). Ethnographic insights on social context and adolescent development among inner-city African-American teens. In R. Jessor, A.Colby, & R. A. Schweder (Eds.), *Ethnography and human development* (pp. 395-418). Chicago: University of Chicago Press.

Cahan Ragan, L. J. (2006). Educating the undocumented: Providing legal status for undocumented students in the United States and Italy through higher education. *Georgia Journal of International and Comparative Law, 34*(2), 485–517.

California Community Colleges (1994). *Transfer: Preparing for the year 2000*. Sacramento: California Community Colleges. (ERIC Document Reproduction Service No. ED371810)

References

Campa, B. (2010). Critical resilience, schooling processes, and the academic success of Mexican Americans in a community college. *Hispanic Journal of Behavioral Sciences, 32*(3), 429-455.

Capps, R., Fix, M., Henderson, E., & Reardon-Anderson, J. (2005). A profile of low-income working immigrant families. *National Survey of America's Families.* Washington, D.C.: The Urban Institute.

Cervantes, R. C., Castro, F. G. (1985). Stress, coping, and Mexican American mental health: A systematic review. *Hispanic Journal of Behavioral Sciences*, 1, 1-73.

Cavazos-Rehg, P. A., Zayas, L. H., & Spitznagel, E. L. (2007). Legal status, emotional well being and subjective health status of Latino immigrants. *Journal of the National Medical Association, 99*, 1126-1131.

Chavez, L. R. (1991). Outside the imagined community: Undocumented settlers and experiences of incorporation. *American Ethnologist, 18*, 257-278.

Chavez, L. R. (1998). *Shadowed lives: Undocumented immigrants in American society* (2nd ed.). Thomson Learning, Inc.

Chávez, L. R. (2001). *Covering immigration: Popular images and the politics of the nation.* Berkeley: University of California Press.

Chávez, L. R. (2008). *The Latino threat: Constructing immigrants, citizens and the nation.* Stanford, CA: Stanford University Press.

Chavez, L. R., Cornelius, W. A., & Jones, O. W. (1986). Utilization of health services by Mexican immigrant women in San Diego. *Journal of Women's Health, 11*(2), 3-20.

Chavez, M. L., Soriano, M., Oliverez, P. (2007). Undocumented students' access to college: The American dream denied. *Latino Studies*, 5, 254–263.

Chavez, L. R, Hubbell, F. A., Mishra, S. I., & Valdez, R. B. (1997). Undocumented Latina immigrants in Orange County, California: A comparative analysis. *International Migration Review, 31*(1), 88–107.

Chronicle of Higher Education (2001, August 21). *Almanac Issue.*

City University of New York. (1995). *Immigration/migration and the CUNY student of the future.* Report prepared by the City University of New York. Author. Cohen, A. M., & Brawer, F. B. (2003). *The American community college.* San Francisco: Jossey-Bass.

Baum, S., Payea, K., Cardenas-Elliott, D. (2010). *Trends in Student Aid 2009-2010.* New York: The College Board.

References

California Tomorrow. (2002). *The high-quality learning conditions needed to support students of color and immigrants at California community colleges: Policy report*. San Francisco: California Tomorrow.

Conchas, G. Q. (2001). Structuring failure and success: Understanding the variability in Latino school engagement. *Harvard Education Review, 70*(3), 475–504.

Conchas, G. Q. (2006). *The color of success: Race and high-achieving urban youth*. New York: Teachers College Press.

Contreras, F. (2009). Sin papeles and rompiendo barreras: Latino college students and the challenges in persisting in college. *Harvard Educational Review, 79*, 610–632.

Contreras, F., Stritikus, T., O'Reilly-Diaz, K., Torres, K., Sanchez, I., Esqueda, M., Ortega, L., & Sepulveda, A. (2008). *Understanding opportunities to learn for Latino students in Washington State*. Report prepared for the Washington State Commission on Hispanic Affairs and the Washington State Legislature. Retrieved August 1, 2009, from http://www.kcts9.org/files/WA%20Latino%20Achievement%20Gap%20Executive%20Summary.pdf

Conye, R. K., & Cook, E. P. (2004). Understanding persons within environments: An introduction to ecological counseling. In R. K. Conye & E. P. Cook (Eds.), *Ecological counseling: An innovative approach to conceptualizing person-environment interaction*. Alexandria, VA: American Counseling Association.

Cornelius, W.A. (1982). Interviewing undocumented immigrants: Methodological reflections based on fieldwork in Mexico and the U.S. *International Migration Review, 16*, 378-411.

Cornelius, W. A., Chavez, L. R., & Jones, O. W. (1984). *Mexican immigration and access to health care*. Center for US-Mexican Studies, UCSD, La Jolla, CA.

De Genova, N. (2002). 'Migrant "Illegality" and Deportability in Everyday Life', *Annual Review of Anthropology 31*, 419-47.

De Leon, S. (2005). *Assimilation and ambiguous experience of the resilient male Mexican immigrants that successfully navigate American higher education*. Unpublished doctoral dissertation: University of Texas Austin.

Diaz-Strong, D., & Meiners, E. (2007). Residents, alien policies, and resistances: Experiences of undocumented Latino students in Chicago's colleges and universities. *InterActions: UCLA Journal of Education and Information Studies, 3*, 1–20.

Dougherty, K. (1992). Community colleges and baccalaureate attainment. *Journal of Higher Education, 63*(2), 188–214.

Dougherty, K. (1994). *The contradictory college: The conflicting origins, impacts, and futures of the community college.* Albany: State University of New York Press.

Dougherty, K. J. (2002). The evolving role of the community college: Policy issues and research questions. In J. C. Smart & W. G. Tierney (Eds.), *Higher education: Handbook of theory and research* (Vol. 17). New York: Agathon.

Dowd, A. C., Bensimon, E. M., Gabbard, G., Singleton, S., Macias, E., Dee, J., et al. (2006). *Transfer access to elite colleges and universities in the United States: Threading the needle of the American dream.* Retrieved June 28, 2009, from www.jackkentcookefoundation.org

Dozier, S. B. (1993). Emotional concerns of undocumented and out-of-status foreign students. *Community Review, 13,* 33–29.

Dozier, S. B. (1995). Undocumented immigrant students at an urban community college: A demographic and academic profile. *Migration World, 13*(1 & 2), 20–22.

Dozier, S. B. (2001). Undocumented and documented international students: A comparative study of their academic profile. *Community College Review, 29*(2), 45-53.

Dumon, W. A. (1983). Effects of undocumented migration for individuals concerned. *International Migration, 21,* 218-229.

Erikson, E. (1997). *The Life Cycle Completed.* New York, NY: W.W. Norton

Escobar, J. I., Hoyos Nervi, C., & Gara, M. A. (2000). Immigration and mental health: Mexican Americans in the United States. *Harvard Review of Psychiatry, 8*(2), 64–72.

Escobar, W., Lozano, H. A., Inzunza, F. (2008). Improving Dreams, Equality, Access, and Success (IDEAS). In G. Madera and others (eds.), *Underground Undergrads: UCLA Undocumented Immigrant Students Speak Out.* Los Angeles: UCLA Center for Labor Research and Education.

Esses, V. M., Dovidio, J. F., Jackson, L. M., & Armstrong, T. L. (2001). The immigration dilemma: The role of perceived group competition, ethnic prejudice, and national identity. *Journal of Social Issues, 57*(3), 389–412.

Evans, G. W., & English, K. (2002). The Environment of Poverty: Multiple stressor exposure, psychophysiological stress, and socioemotional adjustment. *Child Development, 73*(4), 1238–1248.

References

Farley, T., Galves, A., Dickinson, M., & Diaz Pérez, M. (2005). Stress, coping, and health: A comparison of Mexican immigrants, Mexican-Americans, and non-Hispanic Whites. *Journal of Immigrant Health, 7*(3), 213–220.

Fields, R. R. (1962). *The community college movement.* New York: McGraw-Hill.

Finch, B. K., Kolody, B., & Vega, W. A. (2000). Perceived Discrimination and Depression among Mexican-Origin Adults in California. *Journal of Health and Social Behavior, 41*(3), 295–313.

Finch, B. K., & Vega, W. A. (2003). Acculturation stress, social support, and self-related health among Latinos in California. *Journal of Immigrant Health, 5*(3), 109–117.

Fortuny, K., Capps, R., Passel, J. S. (2007). *The Characteristics of Unauthorized Immigrants in California, Los Angeles County, and the United States.* Washington, DC: The Urban Institute.

Frome, P., & Eccles, J. (1998). Parents' influence on children's achievement-related perceptions. *Journal of Personality and Social Psychology, 74*(2), 435-452.

Fry, R. (2002). *Latinos in higher education: Many enroll, too few graduate.* Washington, DC: Pew Hispanic Center.

Fry, R. (2004). *Latino youth finishing college: The role of selective pathways.* Washington, DC: Pew Hispanic Center.

Fuligini, A. (1997). The academic achievement of adolescents from immigrant families: The roles of family background, attitudes, and behavior. *Child Development, 69*(2), 351-363.

Gall, M. D., Gall, J. P., & Borg, W. R. (2003). *Educational research: An introduction* (7th ed.). New York: Longman.

Gallimore, R., & Reese, L. J. (1999). Mexican immigrants in urban California: Forging adaptations from familiar and new cultural resources. In M. C. Foblets & C. L. Pang (Eds.), *Culture, Ethnicity and Immigration* (pp. 245–263). ACCO: Leuven, Belgium.

Gándara, P. (2005). *Fragile futures: Risk and vulnerability among Latino high achievers.* Policy Information Report. Princeton, NJ: ETS.

Gándara, P. & Contreras, F. (2009). *The Latino Education Crisis: The Consequences of Failed Social Policies.* Harvard University Press.

Garcia, R. J. (1995). Critical race theory and Proposition 187: The racial politics of immigration law. *Chicano-Latino Law Review, 17*, 1–28.

Garcia Coll, C., & Magnuson, K. (2005). The psychological experience of immigration: A developmental perspective. In M. M. Suarez-Orozco, C.

Suarez-Orozco, & D. Baolian Qin (Eds.), *The new immigration: An interdisciplinary reader* (pp. 105-133). New York: Brunner-Routledge.

Garcia Coll, C., & Magnuson, K. (2005). The psychological experience of immigration: A developmental perspective. In M. M. Suarez-Orozco, C. Suarez-Orozco, & D. Baolian-Qin (Eds.), *The new immigration: An interdisciplinary reader* (pp. 105-133). New York, NY: Routledge.

Garza, C., & Landeck, M. (2004). College freshman at risk-social problems at issue: An exploratory study of a Texas/Mexico border community college. *Social Science Quarterly, 85*(5), 1390-1400.

Garza, E., Reyes P., & Trueba, E. (2004). *Resiliency and success: Migrant children in the United States.* Boulder Colorado: Paradigm Publishers.

Gee, G. C., Ryan, A., Laflamme, D. J., & Holt, J. (2006). Self-reported discrimination and mental health status among African descendants, Mexican-Americans, and other Latinos in the New Hampshire REACH 2010 Initiative: The added dimension of immigration. *American Journal of Public Health, 96*(10), 1821-1828.

Geertz, C. (1973). "Thick Description: Toward an Interpretive Theory of Culture." In *The Interpretation of Cultures.* Basic Books.

Gildersleeve, R. E. (2009). Organizing learning for transformation in college outreach programmes. *Pedagogies: An International Journal, 4*(1), 77-93.

Gildersleeve, R. E., & Ranero, J. J. (2010). Precollege contexts of undocumented students: Implications for student affairs professionals. *New Directions for Student Services, 131,* 19-33.

Gildersleeve, R. E., Rumann, C., & Mondragón, R. (2010). Serving undocumented students: current law and policy. *New Directions for Student Services, 131,* 5-18.

Gonzales, R. G. (2007). Wasted talent and broken dreams: The lost potential of undocumented students. *Immigration Policy in Focus, 5*(13), 1-11.

Gonzales, R. G. (2008). Left out but not shut down: Political activism and the undocumented student movement. *Northwestern Journal of Law and Social Policy, 3,* 219-239.

Gonzales, R. G. (2010). On the wrong side of the tracks: Understanding the effects of school structure and social capital in the educational pursuits of undocumented immigrant students. *Peabody Journal of Education, 85,* 469-485.

Gonzalez, M. S., Plata, O., Garcia, E., Torres, M., Urrieta, L. (2003). Testimonios de immigrantes: Students educating future teachers. *Journal of Latinos and Education, 2* (4), 233-243.

Grubb, W. N. (1991). The decline of community college transfer rates: Evidence from national longitudinal surveys. *Journal of Higher Education, 62*(2),194–222.

Gutiérrez, K. D., Hunter, J. D., & Arzubiaga, A. (2009). Re-mediating the university: Learning through sociocritical literacies. *Pedagogies: An International Journal, 4*(1), 1-23.

Guttmacher, S. (1983). No golden door: The health care and non-care of the undocumented. *Health PAC Bulletin Quarterly, 14*(2), 15-24.

Hagan, J., & Rodriguez, N. (2002). Resurrecting exclusion: The effects of 1996 immigration reform on families and communities in Texas, Mexico and El Salvador. In M. Suarez-Orozco & M. Paez (Eds.), *Latinos: Remaking America* (pp. 190-201). Los Angeles: University of California Press.

Hagan, J., Rodriguez, N., Capps, R., & Kabiri, N. (2003). Effects of immigration reform on immigrants' access to health care. *International Migration Review, 37*, 444-463.

Hagedorn, L. S., & Cepeda, R. (2004). Serving Los Angeles: Urban community colleges and educational success among Latino students. *Community College Journal of Research and Practice, 28*, 199–211.

Hagedorn, L., Maxwell, W., Chen, A., Cypers, S., & Moon, H. S. (2002). *A community college model of student immigration, language, GPA, and course completion.* Los Angeles: University of Southern California School of Education.

Hall, J. M., Stevens, P. E., & Meleis, A. I. (1994). Marginalization: A guiding concept for valuing diversity in nursing knowledge development. *Advances in Nursing Science, 16*(4), 23-41.

Harvey, W. B. (2003). *Minorities in higher education: Twentieth annual status report,2002–2003.* Washington, DC: American Council on Education.

Hearn, J. (2001). "Access to Postsecondary Education: Financing Equity in an Evolving Context." In M.B. Paulsen and J.C. Smart (Eds.), *The Finance of Higher Education: Theory, Research, Policy and Practice* (pp. 439-460). New York: Agathon Press.

Hernandez, S., Hernandez, I., Gadson, R., Deneece, H., Ortiz, A. M., White, M. C., & Yocum-Gaffney, D. (2010). Sharing their Secrets: Undocumented students' personal stories of fear, drive, and survival. . *New Directions for Student Services, 131*, 67-84.

Herr, E. L. (2004). The context of American life today. In R.K. Conyne & , E. P. Cook (Eds.), *Ecological counseling: An innovative approach to conceptualizing person-environment interaction* (pp. 37-66). Alexandria, VA: American Counseling Association.

Hoachlander, G., Sikora, A. C., Horn, L., & Carroll, C. D. (2003). *Community college students: Goals, academic preparation, and outcomes (NCES 2003-164).* Washington, DC: U.S. Department of Education, National Center for Education Statistics.

Hodgkinson, V. A., & Weitzman, M. S. (1997). *Volunteering and giving among American teenagers 14 to 17 years of age.* Washington, DC: Independent Sector.

Hoefer, M., Rytina, N. Baker, B.C. (2009). *Estimates of the unauthorized immigrant population residing in the United States*: January 2008. Washington, DC: Department of Homeland Security Office of Immigration Statistics.

Holland, A., & Andre, T. (1987). Participation in extracurricular activities in secondary school: What is known, what needs to be known? *Review of Educational Research, 57,* 437–466.

Horn, L., & Nevill, S. (2006). *Profile of undergraduates in U.S. postsecondary education institutions: 2003–04, with a special analysis of community college students* (No. 2006-184). Washington, D.C. : U.S. Department of Education, National Center for Education Statistics.

Horn, L., Nevill, S., & Griffith, J. (2006). *Profile of undergraduates in U.S. postsecondary education institutions, 2003-2004, with special analysis of community college students* (Report No. 2006-184). Washington, DC: NCES Institute of Education Sciences.

Hummer, R. A., Powers, D. A., Pullum, S. G., Gossman, G. L., & Frisbie, W. P. (2007). Paradox found (again): Infant mortality among the Mexican-origin population in the United States. *Demography, 44,* 441–457.

Hurtado, S. H., Saenz, V. B., Santos, J. L., Cabrera, N. L. (2008). *Advancing in higher education: A portrait of Latino College Freshmen at four year institutions, 1975-2006.* Los Angeles: Higher Education Research Institute, UCLA.

Igoa, C. (1995). *The inner world of the immigrant child.* New Jersey: Lawrence Erlbaum Associates.

Jauregui, J. A., Slate, J. R., Stallone, M. (2008). Texas community colleges and characteristics of a growing undocumented student population. *Journal of Hispanic Higher Education, 7*(4), 346-355.

References

Jauregui, J. A., & Slate, J. R. (2009). Texas borderland community colleges and views regarding undocumented students: A qualitative study. *Journal of College Student Retention, 11*(2), 183-210.

Jenkins, D. (2003, March). *The potential of community colleges as bridges to opportunity for the disadvantaged: Can it be achieved on a large scale?* Paper presented at the seminar on Access and Equity for the Community College Research Center, Teachers' College, Columbia University.

Johnston, R. C. (2000a, May 31). Guidance counselors often struggle to help undocumented students. *Education Week.* Retrieved March 21, 2007 from www.edweek.org

Johnston, R. C. (2000b, May 31). Talented, but not legal. *Education Week.* Retrieved March 21, 2007 from www.edweek.org

Jun, A. (2001). *From here to university: Access, mobility, and resilience among urban Latino youth.* New York: Routledge Falmer.

Kao, G. (1999). Psychological well-being and education achievement among immigrant youth. In D. J. Hernandez (Ed.), *Children of immigrant: Health, adjustment and public assistance* (pp. 410–477). Washington, DC: National Academy Press.

Kao, G., & Tienda, M. (1995). Optimism and achievement: The educational performance of immigrant youth. *Social Science Quarterly, 76,*1–19.

Karunanayake, D., & Nauta, M. M. (2004). "The relationship between race and students' identified career role models and perceived role model influence." *Career Development Quarterly, 52,* 225–234.

Keefe, S. E., & Padilla, A. M. (1987). Chicano ethnicity. Albuquerque: University of New Mexico Press.

Kewal Ramani, A., Gilbertson, L., Fox, M., and Provasnik, S. (2007). *Status and trends in the education of racial and ethnic minorities* (NCES 2007–039). National Center for Education Statistics, Institute of Education Sciences, U.S. Department of Education. Washington, DC.

Kintzer, F. C. (1970). *Nationwide pilot study on articulation.* Los Angeles, CA: University of California. (ERIC Document Reproduction Service No. ED045065).

Kintzer, F. C. (1973). *Middleman in higher education.* San Francisco: Jossey-Bass.

Kintzer, F. C. (1996). *An historical and futuristic perspective of articulation and transfer in the United States.* Los Angeles: University of California. (ERIC Document Reproduction Service No. ED389380)

Kintzer, F. C., & Wattenbarger, J. L. (1985). *The articulation/transfer phenomenon: Patterns and directions.* Washington, DC: American Association of Community and Junior Colleges.

Knoell, D. M. (1966). *Toward educational opportunity for all.* Albany: State University of New York.

Knoell, D. M., & Medsker, L. L. (1965). *From junior to senior college: A national study of the transfer student.* Washington, DC: American Council on Education.

Koltai, L. (1981). *The state of the district, 1981.* Los Angeles: Los Angeles Community College District. (ERIC Document Reproduction Service No. ED207654)

Kozol, J. (2005). *The shame of the nation: The restoration of apartheid schooling in America.* New York: Random House.

Kozol, J. (1991). *Savage inequalities: Children in America's schools.* New York: Harper Perennial.

Ku, L., & Waidman, T. (2003). *Kaiser commission on Medicaid and the uninsured, how race/ethnicity, immigration status, and language affect health insurance coverage, access to care and quality of care among the low-income population.* Retrieved December 7, 2004, from http://www.kff.org/uninsured/loader.cfm?url=/commonspot/security/getfile.cfm&PageID=22103.

Kurlaender, M. (2006). Choosing community colleges: Factors affecting Latino college choice. *New Directions for Community Colleges, 133,* 7–16.

Laanan, F. S. (2001). Transfer student adjustment. *New Directions for Community Colleges, 114,* 5-13.

Lanning, P. (2008). The true state of fund raising at two-year colleges. *Community CollegeTimes.* Retrieved Nov. 10, 2008, from http://www.communitycollegetimes.com/articlefm?TopicId=17&ArticleId= 710.

Latinos in education: Early childhood, elementary, secondary, undergraduate, graduate. (1999). Washington, DC: White House Initiative on Educational Excellence for Hispanic Americans.

Lee, W. Y. (2001). Toward a more perfect union: Reflecting on trends and issues for enhancing the academic performance of minority transfer students. *New Directions for Community Colleges, 30*(2), 39-44.

Lee, C.C. (2005). Urban school counseling: Context, characteristics, and competencies. *Professional School Counseling, 8*(3), 184-188.

References

Leovy, J. (2001). When no green card means no college. *Los Angeles Times*, March 24, p. A–1.

Leventhal, T., Xue, Y., & Brooks-Gunn, J. (2006). Immigrant differences in school-age children's verbal trajectories: A look at four racial/ethnic groups. *Child Development, 77,* 1359-1374.

Levitt, P. (2001). *The transnational villagers.* Cambridge, MA: Harvard University Press.

Lombardi, J. (1979). *The decline of transfer education.* Washington, DC: National Institute of Education. (ERIC Document Reproduction Service No. ED179273)

London, H. (1989). Breaking away: A study of first-generation college students and their families. *American Journal of Education, 97*(2), 144–170.

Lopez, N. (2003). *Hopeful girls, troubled boys: Race and gender disparity in urban education.* New York: Routledge.

MacQueen, K. M., McLellan, E., Kay, K., & Millstein, B. (1998). Codebook development for team-based qualitative analysis. *Cultural Anthropology Methods, 10*(2), 31–36.

Martin, S. A. (1999). *Early intervention program and college partnerships.* Washington, DC: George Washington University, School of Education and Human Development.

Martinez, I. (2009). What's age gotta do with it? Understanding the age-identities and school-going practices of Mexican immigrant youth in New York City. *The High School Journal, April/May,* 34-48.

Maxwell, J. A. (2005). Qualitative research design: An interactive approach. *Applied Social Research Methods Series, 41.* Thousand Oaks, CA: Sage Publications, Inc.

McDonough, P. M. (1997). *Choosing colleges: How social class and schools structure opportunity.* Albany: State University of New York Press.

McGrath, D., & Van Buskirk, W. (1999). Cultures of support for at-risk students: The role of social and emotional capital in the educational experiences of women. In Kathleen M. Shaw, James R. Valadez, & Robert A. Rhoads (Eds.), *Community colleges as cultural contexts: Qualitative explorations of organizational and student culture.* Albany, NY: State University of New York Press.

McGuire, S., & Georges, J. (2003). Undocumentedness and liminality as health variables. *Advances in Nursing Science, 26*(3), 185-196.

McMillan, J. H., & Reed, D. F. (1994). At-risk students and resiliency: Factors contributing to academic success, *The Clearing House, 67*(3), 137–140.

Mehta C., & Ali, A. (2003). *Education For All: Chicago's Undocumented Immigrants And Their Access To Higher Education*. Chicago, IL: Center for Urban Economic Development at the University of Illinois.

Messias, D. K. H. (1996). Exploring the concept of undocumentedness: The meaning of a person's immigration status to nursing care. *Scholarly Inquiry for Nursing Practice, 10,* 235-252.

Miksch, K. L. (2005). Legal issues in developmental education: Immigrant students and the DREAM Act. *Research and Teaching in Developmental Education, 22*(1), 59–65.

Miles, M. B., & Huberman, A. M. (1994). *Qualitative data analysis*. San Francisco: Sage.

Miller, K. A. (1985). *Emigrants and exiles: Ireland and the Irish exodus to North America*. New York: Oxford University Press.

Moore, E. (1986). Issues in access to health care: The undocumented Mexican resident in Richmond, California. *Medical Anthropology Quarterly, 17,* 65-70.

Morales, A., Herrera, S., Murry, K. (2009). Navigating the Waves of Social and Political Capriciousness Inspiring Perspectives From DREAM-Eligible Immigrant Students. *Journal of Hispanic Higher Education, 8*(1), 1-18.

Munoz, S. M. (2008). *Understanding issues of college persistence for undocumented Mexican immigrant women from the new Latino Diaspora: A case study*. Unpublished doctoral dissertation: Iowa State University.

National Center for Education Statistics. (2006). *Digest of Education Statistics, 2005*. Washington, DC: Author.

National Immigration Law Center. 2005. *Basic Facts about In-State Tuition for Undocumented Immigrant Students. Los Angeles*: National Immigration Law Center.

Nolin, M. J., Chaney, B., Chapman, C., & Chandler, K. (1997). *Student participation in community service*. Washington, DC: U.S. Department of Education.

Nora, A., & Rendón, L. (1990). Determinants of predisposition to transfer among community college students: A structural model. *Research in Higher Education, 31,* 235–255.

Nora, A., Rendón, L. I., & Cuadraz, G. (1999). Access, choice, and outcomes: A profile of Hispanic students in higher education. In A. Tashakkori & S. H. Ochoa (Eds.), *Education of Hispanics in the United States: Politics, policies, and outcomes* (Vol. 16, Readings on Equal Education.) New York: AMS Press.

Nuñez, A-M., & Carroll, D. (1998). First-generation students: Undergraduates whose parents never enrolled in postsecondary education. Washington, D.C.: U.S. Department of Education.

Oakes, J. (1985). Keeping track: How schools structure inequality. Binghamton, NY: Vail Ballou Press.

Ogbu, J. U. (1991). Immigrant and involuntary minorities in comparative perspective. In J. Ogbu & M. Gibson (Eds.), *Minority Status and Schooling: A Comparative Study of Immigrant and Involuntary Minorities* (3–33). New York: Garland.

Ogbu, J., & Simmons, H.D. (1998). Voluntary and involuntary minorities: A cultural ecological theory of school performance with some implications for education. *Anthropology & Education Quarterly, 29*, 155-188.

Olivas, M. (2004). IIRIRA, the DREAM Act, and undocumented student residency. *Journal of College and University Law, 30*(2), 323–351.

Oliverez, P. M. (2006). *Ready but restricted: An examination of the challenges of college access and financial aid for college-ready undocumented students in the U.S.* Unpublished doctoral dissertation, University of Southern California.

Oliverez, P. M., Chavez, M. L., Soriano, M., & Tierney, W. G. (Eds.). (2006). *The college and financial aid guide for AB 540 undocumented immigrant students* (The AB 540 College Access Network). Los Angeles, CA: University of Southern California, Center for Higher Education Policy Analysis.

Orfield, G., & Yun, J. (1999). *Resegregation in American schools.* Cambridge: Harvard University, The Civil Rights Project.

Ornelas, A., & Solorzano, D. G. (2004). Transfer conditions of Latino community college students: A single institution case study. *Community College Journal of Research and Practice, 28,* 233–248.

Ortiz, A. M., & Hinojosa, A. (2010). Tenuous options: The career development process for undocumented students. *New Directions for Student Services, 131,* 53-65.

Padilla, A. M. (1986). Acculturation and stress among immigrants and later generation individuals. In D. Frick, H. Hoefert, H. Legewie, R. Mackensen, & R. K. Silbereisen (Eds.), *The quality of urban life: Social, psychological, and physical conditions* (pp. 100-120). Berlin, Germany: de Gruyter.

Padilla A.M., Cervantes, R.C., Maldonado, M., Garcia R.E. (1988). Coping responses to psychosocial stressors in Mexican and Central American immigrants. *Journal of Community Psychology, 16*, 418-427.

Padilla, A. M., & Pérez, W. (2003). Acculturation, social identity, and social cognition: A new perspective. *Hispanic Journal of Behavioral Sciences, 25*, 35–55.

Palloni, A., & Morenoff, J. D. (2001). Interpreting the paradoxical in the Hispanic paradox: Demographic and epidemiologic approaches. *Annals of the New York Academy of Sciences, USA, 954*, 140–174.

Pascarella, E., & Terenzini, P. T. (1991) *How college affects students.* San Francisco: Jossey-Bass.

Passel, J., & Cohn, D. (2009). A Portrait of Unauthorized Immigrants in the United States. Washington, DC: Pew Hispanic Center.

Pearson, M. R. (2010). How "undocumented workers" and "illegal aliens" affect prejudice toward Mexican immigrants. *Social Influence, 5*(2), 118-132.

Pérez, M. C., & Fortuna, L. (2005). Psychosocial stressors, psychiatric diagnoses, and utilization of mental health services among undocumented immigrant Latinos. *Journal of Immigrant and Refugee Services, 3*, 107-123.

Pérez, P. (1999). *Development of a mentor program for Latino students at Borough of Manhattan Community College.* Ed.D. Practicum Paper, Nova Southeastern University, Ft. Lauderdale, FL.

Pérez, W. (2009). *We ARE Americans: Undocumented students pursuing the American dream.* Sterling, VA: Stylus Publishing.

Pérez, W. (2004). Mexican heritage adolescents' social comparisons and their academic achievement: Testing the dual frame of reference hypothesis. (Doctoral dissertation, Stanford University, 2004). *UMI Dissertation Publishing No. 3128682.*

Pérez, W., Cortés, R., Ramos, K., & Coronado, H. (2010). Cursed and blessed: Examining the socioemotional and academic experiences of undocumented Latino/a college students. *New Directions for Student Services, 131*, 35-51.

Pérez, W., Espinoza, R., Ramos, K., Coronado, H, Cortés, R. (2009). Academic Resilience Among Undocumented Latino Students. *Hispanic Journal of Behavioral Sciences, 31(2), 149-181.*

Pérez, W., Espinoza, R., Ramos, K., Coronado, H., & Cortés, R. (2010). Civic

References

engagement patterns of undocumented Mexican students. *Journal of Hispanic Higher Education, 9(3), 245-265.*

Pérez, W., Munoz, S., Alcantar, C., Guarneros, N. (In Press). Educators supporting DREAMERS: Becoming an Undocumented Student Ally. In Landsman, J. & Lewis, C. W. (Eds). *White Teachers/Diverse Classrooms: A Guide to Building Inclusive Schools, Promoting High Expectations, and Eliminating Racism (2nd Edition).* Sterling, VA: Stylus Publishing.

Pérez, W., Ramos, K., Coronado, H., & Cortés, R. D. (2006). *Loss of talent: High achieving undocumented students in the U.S.* Symposium presented at the Annual Association for the Study of Higher Education Conference, Anaheim, CA.

Pérez, W., Ramos, K., Coronado, H., & Cortés, R. D. (2007). *Developing talent: Strategies for supporting high-achieving community college students.* Symposium presented at 4th Annual Tomas Rivera Policy Institute Education Conference, Long Beach, CA.

Pérez Huber, L. & Malagon, M. C. (2007). Silenced struggles: The experiences of Latina and Latino undocumented college students in California. *Nevada Law Journal, 7,* 841-861.

Perry, A. M. (2006). Toward a theoretical framework for membership: The case of undocumented immigrants and financial aid for postsecondary education. *The Review of Higher Education, 30*(1), 21–40.

Pew Hispanic Center. (2009, April). *A portrait of unauthorized immigrants in the United States.* Washington, DC: Pew Hispanic Center.

Phillippe, K. A., & Sullivan, L. G. (2005). *National profile of community colleges: Trends and statistics* (4th ed.). Washington, DC: Community College Press.

Phinney, J. S., Horenczyk, G., Liebkind, K., & Vedder, P. (2001). Ethnic identity, immigration, and well-being: An interactional perspective. *Journal of Social Issues, 57*(3), 493-510.

Pickwell, S. M., & Warnock, F. (1994). Family nurse practitioner faculty clinical practice with undocumented migrants. *Family Community Health, 16*(4), 32-38.

Pincus, F. L. (1980). The false promises of community colleges: Class conflict and vocational education. *Harvard Educational Review, 50,* 332–361.

Pincus, F. L., & Archer, E. (1989). *Bridges to opportunity? Are community colleges meeting the transfer needs of minority students?* New York: College Board.

Plyler, Superintendent, Tyler Independent School District, et al. v. Doe, Guargian, et al., 457 202 (1982).

Ponce, N., Nordyke, R. J., and Hirota, S. (2005). Uninsured working immigrants: A view from a California county. *Journal of Immigrant Health, 7*(1), 45–53.

Portes, A. (1995). Children of Immigrants: Segmented Assimilation and Its Determinants. In A. Portes (Ed.), *The economic sociology of immigration: essays on networks, ethnicity, and entrepreneurship*, (pp. 248–279). New York: Russell Sage.

Portes, A., & Rumbaut, R. G. (2001). *Legacies: The store of the immigrant second generation*. Berkeley, CA: The University of California Press.

Portes, A., & Rumbaut, R. G. (2006). *Immigration America* (3rd ed.). Berkeley, CA: University of California Press.

Potochnick, S. R., & Perreira, K. M. (2010). Depression and anxiety among first-generation immigrant Latino youth: Key correlates and implications for future research. *The Journal of Nervous and Mental Disease, 198*(7), 470-477.

Rendón, L. (1994). Validating culturally diverse students: Toward a new model of learning and student development. *Innovative Higher Education, 19*, 33–51.

Rifkin, T. (Ed.). (1996). Transfer and articulation policies: Implications for practice. In T. Rifkin (Ed.), *Transfer and articulation: Improving policies to meet new needs*. New Directions for Community Colleges, No. 96 (pp. 35–43). San Francisco: Jossey-Bass.

Rincón, A. (2008). *Undocumented Immigrants and Higher Education: Sí se Puede!* New York: LFB Scholarly Publishing.

Rivera, F. I. (2007). Contexualizing the experience of young Latino adults: Acculturation, social support, and depression. *Journal of Immigrant and Minority Health, 9*, 237–244.

Rodriguez, N., & Hagan, J. (2004). Fractured families and communities: Effects of immigration reform in Texas, Mexico, and El Salvador. *Latino Studies, 2*, 328-351.

Roeser, R.W., Eccles, J.S., & Strobel, K.R. (1998). Linking the study of schooling and mental health: Selected issues and empirical illustrations at the level of the individual. *Educational Psychologist, 33*(3), 153-176.

Rogers, J., Saunders, M., Terriquez, V., & Velez, V. (2008). Civic lessons: Public schools and the civic development of undocumented students and parents. *Northwestern Journal of Law and Social Policy, 3*, 201-218.

Romano, J. C., Gallagher, G., & Shugart, S. C. (2010). More than an open door: Deploying philanthropy to student access and success in American community colleges. *New Directions for Student Services, 130*, 55-70.

Rumbaut, R. G., & Komaie, G. (2010). Immigration and adult transitions. *The Future of Children, 20*(1), 43-66.

Rutter, M. (1988). Stress, coping, and development: Some issues and some questions. In N. Garmezy & M. Rutter (Eds.), *Stress, coping, and development in children* (pp. 1–41). Baltimore, MD: The Johns Hopkins University Press.

Salinas, A., & Llanes, J. R. (2003). Student attrition, retention, and persistence: the case of the University of Texas–Pan American. *Journal of Hispanic Higher Education, 2*, 73-97.

Santa Ana, O. (2002). *Brown tide rising: Metaphors of Latinos in contemporary American public discourse.* Austin: University of Texas Press.

Santrock, J. W. (1997). *Life-span development* (6th ed.). Madison, WI: Brown & Benchmark.

Schlossberg, Nancy K. (1989) Marginality and mattering: Key issues in building community. In D. C. Roberts (Ed.), *Designing campus activities to foster a sense of community* (New Directions for Student Services, No. 48, pp. 5–15). San Francisco: Jossey-Bass.

Schuetz, P. (2005). UCLA community college review: Campus environment: A missing link in studies of community college attrition. *Community College Review, 32*(4), 60-80.

Simich, L. (2006). Hidden meanings of health security: Migration experiences and systemic barriers to mental well-being among non-status migrants in Canada. *International Journal of Migration Health and Social Care, 2*, 16-27.

Smart, J. F. & Smart, D. W. (1995). Acculturative stress of Hispanics: Loss and challenge. *Journal of Counseling and Development, 73*, 390-396.

Solarzano D., Ceja, M. & Yosso, T. (2000). Critical race theory, racial microagressions, and campus racial climate: The experience of African American college students. *Journal of Negro Education, 69*(1/2), pp. 60–73.

Souto-Manning, M. (2007) Immigrant families and children (re)develop identities in a new context. *Early Childhood Education Journal, 34*(6), 399–405.

References

Stanton-Salazar, R. D. (2001). *Manufacturing hope and despair: The school and kin support networks of U.S.-Mexican Youth.* New York: Teachers College Press.

Stanton-Salazar, R. D., & Dornbusch, S. M. (1995). Social capital and the reproduction of inequality: Information networks among Mexican-origin high school students. *Sociology of Education, 68*(2), 116–135.

Strauss, A., & Corbin, J. M. (1990). *Basics of qualitative research: Grounded theory procedures and techniques.* Newbury Park, CA: Sage.

Suarez, A. L. (2003). Forward transfer: Strengthening the education pipeline for Latino community college students. *Community College Journal of Research and Practice, 27,* 95–117.

Suarez-Orozco, M.M. (1989). *Central American refugees and U.S. High schools: A psychosocial study of motivation and achievement.* Stanford: Stanford University Press.

Suarez-Orozco, C. (2001a). Afterword: Understanding and serving the children of immigrants. *Harvard Educational Review, 71*(3), 579–589.

Suarez-Orozco, C. (2001b). Identities under siege: Immigration stress and social mirroring among the children of immigrants. In M. M. Suarez-Orozco, C. Suarez-Orozco, & D. Baolian Qin (Eds.), *The new immigration: An interdisciplinary reader* (pp. 135–155). New York: Brunner-Routledge.

Suarez-Orozco, C. (2005). Identities under siege: Immigration stress and social mirroring among the children of immigrants. In M. M. Suarez-Orozco, C. Suarez-Orozco, & D. Baolian-Qin (Eds.), *The new immigration: An interdisciplinary reader* (pp. 105–133). New York: Routledge.

Suarez-Orozco, C., & Suarez-Orozco, M. M. (1995). *Transformation: Migration, family life, and achievement motivation among Latino adolescents.* Stanford, CA: Stanford University Press.

Suarez-Orozco, C., & Suarez-Orozco, M. M. (2001). *Children of immigration.* Cambridge, MA: Harvard University Press.

Sullivan, M. M., & Rehm, R. (2005). Mental health of undocumented Mexican immigrants: A review of the literature. *Advances Nursing Science., 28,* 240-251.

Summers, M. D. (2003). ERIC review: Attrition research at community colleges. *Community College Review, 30*(4), 64-84.

Super, D. E. (1984). Career and life development. In D. Brown and L. Brooks (eds.), *Career Choice and Development: Applying Contemporary Theories to Practice.* San Francisco: Jossey-Bass.

Szelényi, K., and Chang, J. C. (2002). Educating immigrants: The community college role. *Community College Review, 30*(2), 55–73.

Swail, W. S., Cabrera, A. F., & Lee, C. (2004). *Latino youth and the pathway to college*. Washington, DC: Pew Hispanic Center.

Tornatzky, L. G., Cutler, R., & Lee, J. (2002). *College knowledge: What Latino parents need to know and why they don't know it*. Los Angeles: Tomás Rivera Policy Institute at the University of Southern California.

University of California, Davis. (2008). *UC Davis guide for unauthorized immigrant students: FAQ about Assembly Bill 540*. University of California Office of the President.

Ureta, C. G. (2001). *A case study of the psychology of an undocumented Mexican woman immigrant*. Unpublished doctoral dissertation: University of California, Berkeley.

U.S. Department of Education (2003). *The condition of education, 2003* (NCES 2003-067). Washington, DC: U.S. Government Printing Office.

U.S. Department of Homeland Security. (2009). *Yearbook of immigration statistics:2008*.Washington, DC: U.S. Department of Homeland Security, Office of Immigration Statistics.

Valdés, G. (1996). *Con Respeto: Bridging the distances between culturally diverse families and schools: an ethnographic portrait*. New York: Teachers College Columbia University.

Valenzuela, A. (2003). "Desde entonces, soy Chicana": A Mexican immigrant student resists subtractive schooling. In M. Sadowski (Ed.), *Adolescents at school* (pp. 50–54). Cambridge, MA: Harvard Education Press.

Walcott, H. F. (1990). *Writing up qualitative research*. Beverly Hills, CA: Sage Publications, Inc.

Wang, M.C., Haertel, G.D., & Walberg, H.J. (1994). Educational resilience in inner cities. In M.C. Wang & E.W. Gordon (Eds.), *Educational resilience in inner-city America: Challenges and prospects*. Hillsdale, NJ: Erlbaum.

Wassmer, R., Moore, C., & Shulock, N. (2004). Effect of racial/ethnic composition on transfer rates in community colleges: Implications for policy and practice. *Research in Higher Education, 45*, 651–672.

Weintraub, S. (2003). Illegal immigrants in Texas: Impact on social services and related considerations. *International Migration Review, 18*, 733-747.

Wellman, J. V. (2002). *State policy and community college-baccalaureate* (National Center Report, No. 02-6). Washington, DC: National Center for Public Policy and Higher Education and the Institute for Higher Education Policy.

Wells, A. S., & Serna, I. (1996). The Politics of Culture: Understanding Local Political Resistance to Detracking in Racially Mixed Schools. *Harvard Educational Review, 66*(1), 93-118.

Witt, A. A., Wattenbarger, J. L., Gollanttscheck, J. F., & Suppiger, J. E. (1994). *America's community colleges: The first century.* Washington, DC: American Association of Community Colleges.

Yates, L. S. (2004). Plyler v. Doe and the rights of undocumented immigrants to higher education: Should undocumented students be eligible for in-state college tuition rates? *Washington University Law Quarterly, 82,* 585-609.

Youniss, J., McCLellan, J. A., & Mazer, B. (2001). Voluntary service, peer group orientation, and civic engagement. *Journal of Adolescent Research, 16(5),* 456-468.

Zamani, E. M. (2001). Institutional responses to barriers to the transfer process. In F. S. Laanan (Ed.), *Transfer students: Trends and issues.* New Directions for Community Colleges, No. 114 (pp. 15–24). San Francisco: Jossey-Bass.

Zea, M. C., Diehl, V. A., & Porterfield, K. S. (1997). Central American youth exposed to war violence. In J. Garcia and M. C. Zea (Eds.), *Psychological Interventions and Research with Latino Populations* (pp. 39–55). Needham Heights, MA: Allyn & Bacon.

Zhou, M. (1997). Growing up American: The challenge of immigrant children and children of immigrants. *Annual Review of Sociology, 23,* 63-95.

Zuniga, M. E. (2002). Latino immigrants: Patterns of survival. *Journal of Human Behavior in the Social Environment, 5*(3), 137–155.

Index

AB540, 42, 54, 61, 91, 92, 93, 94, 96, 99, 100, 101, 102, 103, 105
Academic Self-Efficacy, 41, 67, 186
access to higher education, 7, 15, 109, 111, 116, 129, 131
acculturation, 9, 12, 16, 17, 18, 20
acculturative stress, 17, 18, 19
achievement, 23, 27, 28, 29, 30, 31, 32, 33, 36, 65, 67, 80, 82, 108, 121, 122, 130, 138, 139, 142, 147, 150
achievement motivation, 23, 32, 36, 67
adversity, 15, 63, 68
advocates, 7, 8, 15, 88, 98, 99, 102, 103, 105, 107, 112
anti-immigrant, 3, 4, 14, 22, 52, 54, 62, 84, 118, 119, 124, 130
anti-immigrant sentiment, 4, 14, 52, 62, 118, 130
anxiety, 12, 14, 15, 17, 21, 22, 32, 33, 38, 52, 107, 115, 116, 148
bilingual, 36, 44, 115
bilingualism, 36, 39
border agents, 21
career choice, 31
career development, 31, 113, 146

Central American, 20, 146, 150, 152
community college, 1, 2, 12, 13, 14, 24, 26, 27, 29, 30, 33, 34, 37, 38, 44, 46, 48, 49, 50, 51, 52, 55, 58, 59, 61, 62, 65, 67, 68, 69, 72, 73, 74, 75, 79, 81, 84, 85, 87, 88, 90, 91, 93, 95, 96, 103, 105, 106, 110, 111, 119, 120, 123, 124, 134, 135, 136, 137, 138, 139, 140, 141, 142, 145, 146, 149, 150, 151, 152
community colleges, 5, 13, 14, 24, 25, 26, 27, 28, 30, 46, 58, 74, 87, 93, 101, 106, 108, 111, 112, 115, 118, 120, 123, 134, 136, 140, 142, 143, 147, 148, 149, 151, 152
community service, 11, 145, 155, 156, 158, 160
coping, 20, 38, 63, 77, 123, 136, 138, 149
counselor, 10, 29, 61, 68, 72, 79, 81, 99, *See* institutional agents
counselors, 9, 13, 35, 67, 72, 78, 79, 85, 86, 99, 101, 106, 107,

183

108, 110, 113, 114, 115, 120, 121, 123, 126, 127
deportation, 3, 9, 12, 17, 18, 19, 20, 21, 52, 103, 118
deportations, 3, 20
depression, 9, 15, 16, 17, 19, 20, 22, 32, 33, 38, 41, 51, 52, 63, 115, 121, 148
discrimination, 5, 12, 13, 14, 16, 18, 19, 20, 22, 23, 32, 33, 38, 41, 48, 55, 56, 57, 62, 81, 118, 121, 123, 133, 139, 162, 163
distress, 12, 15, 20, 21, 33, 36, 38, 48, 55, 57, 88, 116
DREAM Act, 8, 129, 130, 145, 146
dual frame of reference, 23, 122, 147
Enforcement, 5, 21
English language proficiency, 33, 39
English proficiency, 18, 29, 40, 44, 56, 65
faculty, 13, 15, 27, 35, 67, 84, 98, 107, 110, 114, 115, 120
family separation, 20
fear, 1, 3, 9, 10, 12, 17, 18, 19, 20, 21, 22, 30, 32, 33, 34, 38, 50, 51, 52, 88, 89, 91, 94, 104, 106, 110, 115, 118, 121, 134, 141
financial aid, 1, 5, 7, 8, 13, 14, 29, 30, 31, 49, 50, 58, 59, 86, 93, 100, 107, 109, 110, 111, 121, 124, 125, 146, 147
gangs, 4, 77, 78, 119
guilt, 19, 33, 88, 89
high schools, 28, 35, 69, 95, 116

Homeland Security, 5, 20, 141, 151
identity, 4, 9, 10, 22, 23, 35, 36, 37, 109, 114, 121, 135, 138, 146, 148
illegal aliens, 1, 4
immigrant population, 3
immigrants, 1, 2, 3, 4, 5, 6, 8, 15, 16, 17, 18, 19, 20, 21, 22, 23, 27, 28, 90, 112, 122, 128, 130, 131
immigration, 3, 4, 6, 7, 8, 9, 17, 18, 19, 20, 21, 24, 29, 33, 34, 35, 41, 49, 51, 54, 56, 73, 79, 85, 90, 98, 109, 114, 127, 128, 129, 130, 136, 137, 138, 139, 140, 141, 143, 145, 148, 149, 150, 151
Immigration and Control Enforcement, 3
immigration law, 20, 139
immigration laws, 20
immigration policies, 3, 24, 34, 114, 128
immigration reform, 7, 8, 130, 140, 149
In-depth interviews, 37
in-state tuition, 5, 8, 101, 111, 124, 125, 128, 129
institutional agents, 24, 34, 65, 68, 107, 108
institutional commitment, 30, 34
institutional support, 29, 115, 124
Latino students, 1, 11, 12, 13, 15, 24, 26, 27, 33, 34, 35, 38, 55, 62, 66, 69, 79, 84, 87, 118, 119, 123, 124, 130, 137, 141, 147

Index

legal barriers, 31
legal status, 2, 3, 9, 11, 12, 15, 17, 18, 20, 31, 32, 38, 41, 55, 56, 61, 62, 79, 82, 85, 118, 120, 121, 123, 125, 129, 131, 135
marginalization, 8, 12, 14, 19, 33, 57, 118
marginalized, 1, 17, 32, 105, 121
mental health, 16, 18, 21, 33, 133, 134, 136, 138, 139, 147, 149
Mexicans, 3, 10
Mexico, 3, 7, 29, 38, 43, 65, 137, 139, 140, 142, 149, 178, 179
mixed status families, 21
mixed-status families, 22
Motivation, 42, 75, 188
optimism, 10, 24, 32, 38, 57, 63, 85, 123
parental involvement, 10
Plyler v. Doe, 6, 7, 128, 130
police, 20, 21
postsecondary education, 7, 24, 29, 30, 109, 125, 141, 145, 147
poverty, 2, 3, 10, 12, 21, 32, 112, 126, 128, 131
prejudice, 2, 4, 23, 27, 52, 57, 91, 138, 147, 162
professional development, 15, 114, 116, 124
protective factors, 20, 38, 123
raids, 3, 5, 20, 21
recruitment, 13, 35, 106, 108, 113, 124
resilience, 31, 85, 104, 120, 126, 135, 142, 151
retention, 13, 31, 87, 113, 134, 149

scholarships, 1, 24, 49, 50, 51, 58, 60, 65, 72, 73, 81, 84, 96, 98, 100, 110, 118, 121, 184
SES, 26
shame, 10, 19, 33, 50, 51, 88, 89, 118, 143
social isolation, 17
social mobility, 4
social security number, 30, 49, 62, 70, 96, 107
social support, 15, 18, 20, 38, 63, 73, 106, 120, 138, 148
socioemotional challenges, 2, 5, 12, 13, 14, 15, 18, 28, 32, 33, 34, 38, 41, 55, 62, 79, 90, 91, 115, 118, 123
socioemotional experiences, 88, 138
stereotypes, 10, 77
stress, 10, 12, 14, 17, 18, 19, 20, 107, 115, 133, 138, 146, 149, 150
stressors, 8, 9, 10, 18, 21, 63, 77, 146, 147
substance abuse, 16, 20
suicide, 16
transfer, 25, 26, 27, 28, 46, 72, 84, 95, 98, 99, 108, 120, 134, 140, 143, 144, 145, 148, 150, 151, 152
trust, 34, 89, 98, 107, 109
tuition, 1, 5, 7, 8, 14, 24, 25, 58, 59, 60, 62, 72, 80, 81, 87, 91, 92, 94, 100, 101, 102, 103, 105, 110, 111, 112, 118, 120, 124, 125, 128, 129, 152
undocumented students, xi, 2, 4, 5, 6, 7, 8, 9, 10, 11, 12, 13, 14,

24, 28, 29, 30, 31, 32, 33, 34, 35, 37, 38, 42, 44, 46, 49, 50, 54, 55, 56, 58, 59, 61, 62, 63, 65, 69, 71, 72, 73, 74, 75, 80, 84, 85, 86, 87, 89, 90, 91, 92, 93, 94, 95, 96, 97, 98, 99, 100, 101, 102, 103, 104, 105, 106, 107, 108, 109, 110, 111, 112, 113, 114, 115, 116, 118, 119, 120, 123, 124, 125, 126, 127, 128, 129, 130, 131, 133, 135, 140, 142, 146, 149, 152, 183, 184, 185

University of California, 1, 6, 13, 86, 133, 136, 140, 143, 148, 151

CPSIA information can be obtained at www.ICGtesting.com
Printed in the USA
LVOW08*2355300816

502577LV00003B/3/P

9 781593 324612